WALKING IN
NORTHERN FRANCE

Martin Collins

MPC
HUNTER
PUBLISHING INC

British Library
Cataloguing in Publication Data

Collins, Martin, *1941-*
  Walking in Northern France.
  1. Walking — France, Northern —
  Guide-books
  2. France, Northern — Description
  and travel — Guide-books
  I. Title
  796.5'1'09442   GV199..44.F7

Published by
Moorland Publishing Co Ltd,
Moor Farm Road, Airfield Estate,
Ashbourne, Derbyshire,
DE6 1HD England

ISBN 0 86190 160 6 (paperback)
ISBN 0 86190 161 4 (hardback)

Published in the USA by
Hunter Publishing Inc,
300 Raritan Centre Parkway,
CN94, Edison, NJ 08818

1SBN 0 935161 63

Printed in the UK by
Butler and Tanner Ltd, Frome

The illustrations were taken by
Martin Collins, except those on
pages 20, 32, 33, 39, 44, 51,
54, 57, 59, 66, 78, 84, 86, 89,
90, 93, 96, 102, 112, 113, 128,
131, 143, 154, 156, 157, 165,
169, 173, 186, 188, which were
supplied by the French Government Tourist Office.
The sketch maps were drawn by
the author.
Cover; The cliff path at Etretat
(Martin Collins)

Acknowledgement
The author would like to thank
Sally Collins for help with the
French language.

Contents

Introduction

About this guide

When visiting a large country like France, it is all too easy to overlook local possibilities for exploring the countryside on foot. Specialist walking guides either tend to address themselves to the committed long-distance hiker who is prepared to carry a bulky rucksack and overnight in hostel or tent, or they cater for people heading for the Alps or Pyrenees, France's premier regions for the serious walker.

It is equally true, of course, that many holidaymakers wish to do no more than take the occasional stroll round a town or along a beach. Others still will choose to pursue activities and sports which leave little time or inclination for walking.

There is, however, a middle ground, a broad category of visitors to France who, while not devotees of hiking as such, nevertheless enjoy a good ramble of modest length which can be built into a programme of varied holiday activities. Almost without exception, walking provides the best framework for exploration. Impressions of the landscape and its people are intimate, glimpses gained of wildlife are more rewarding, while the unexpected can often bring humour and colour to an outing. There is a very real sense in which local people respond more openly and with greater warmth to the passing walker: touring by car isolates and removes us from contact with the real countryside.

Arriving at a selection of short walks in northern France is rather like suggesting recommended reading for a student of the English language: the choice is almost overwhelming, the permutations endless, the result inevitably tinged with personal preference. In fact, whatever one's destination, numerous footpaths will be encountered, since the French nation enjoys the great outdoors and walking appears high on a list of favourite activities. The country is criss-crossed by a network of long-distance footpaths — *sentiers de grandes randonnées,* 'GR' for short — each of which is allocated a number and maintained by voluntary helpers. There are also countless kilometres of field paths, ancient tracks, canal and river towpaths and quiet country lanes which see virtually no traffic.

Problems for foreign visitors arise, however, when walks are sought which will take them a little further afield, introducing them to places of interest in a region without requiring expensive, specialist walking gear or a high level of physical fitness. Unless purchasing large-scale maps or French-language guides, with an ability to read both, visitors to an area may be reluctant to embark upon paths of unknown length, terrain and duration, thus passing up many opportunities for worthwhile expeditions.

This book aims to redress the balance, albeit incompletely, by offering a total of sixty-six short to medium distance day-walks, distributed round seven centres in northern France. In many ways it is a scratching of the surface of possibilities, as many volumes this size would be required to form a comprehensive survey. However, the reader can rest assured that the areas and individual walks chosen for this book are all of sound quality and represent some of France's very finest country.

How to use this guide

The seven centres selected for the walks are spread across northern France from the Ardennes and Vosges in the east, through Ile de France near Paris, the Normandy coast and interior, to Brittany in the west. Most centres have ten walks, one or two a few less. Each walk is headed by the places at which it starts and finishes, along with those passed en route. The majority of walks are circular. Just below appears the distance in kilometres and approximate duration in hours (based on a leisurely pace but not including halts for meals, extended sightseeing, photography, etc). There follows a summary of the walk's character in a sentence or so, facilitating choice of routes at a glance.

Walks vary in length from 3 or 4km strolls suitable for all the family, up to respectable day-long rambles of 18km or thereabouts. Average length is about 12km ($7^1/_2$ miles), a half-day excursion of 3 to 4 hours.

In describing the walks, route directions often take precedence over the scenery, though viewpoints and features of note are always mentioned. Path routings do change from time to time owing to the interests of farming, forestry, road building and land ownership, which no guide can anticipate. Where this occurs, waymarking on the ground usually clarifies points of doubt on the printed page.

On most routes, a 1:50,000 or 1:25,000 map (purchased in the local area or back home prior to departure) is a handy back-up if the weather deteriorates and a retreat becomes necessary, or if other circumstances dictate short-cutting the walk. In the Vosges mountains and the Ardennes forests, a compass will reassure if lack of visibility due to low cloud or trees is causing concern. Paths, however, are generally well-signed and this guidebook's own sketchmaps have been specially prepared to scale, so that a quick and convenient check on progress can be made at any time.

What to take on the walks

Specialised clothing and equipment is unnecessary for the very short walks, but for the longer ones, sensible outdoor wear is advisable: waterproofs, spare sweater, comfortable footwear with good tread pattern. A little high-energy food such as chocolate or sweets is useful to have in reserve for the unexpected delay.

Much depends on the season and the weather

conditions prevailing   at the time the walks are undertaken: a pleasant amble in summer sunshine can turn into a struggle against wind and driving rain during storms (especially on the coast), with dry paths becoming slippery and muddy. Less pleasant weather and shorter hours of daylight in late autumn and winter will dictate the carrying of more protective clothing, rations and a torch. Common sense and a weather eye — preferably a forecast — will usually suffice, and in any case, shelter is frequently near at hand.

Local tourist information offices (*Syndicat d'Initiative* or *Office de Tourisme*) often provide leaflets on notable buildings, waymarked trails, local beauty spots and amenities which can add greatly to the value of a walk by illuminating the area's history, customs, ecology and features of special interest.

Except on the shortest walks when, perhaps, little will need to be carried, a lightweight rucksack forms the ideal receptacle for all the above bits and pieces, in addition to other items such as this book, a camera, binoculars and picnic. A map-case, while not essential, protects maps from rain and excessive wear and tear.

NOTE FOR WALKERS: Unlike Britain, which is at present free from rabies, this dangerous disease is present in France and can be transmitted to humans by an infected animal. While the chance of this occurring are very slim indeed, it is advisable to avoid physical contact with wild creatures encountered during these walks, whatever the circumstances.

1 Hautes-Vosges

How to get there

Nearest airports: Strasbourg, Colmar and Mulhouse.

Rail: Frequent and fast links from Paris (Gare-de-l'Est) to Strasbourg, Colmar and Mulhouse, with good local bus and train services.

Road: A4 Autoroute east from Paris to Strasbourg. The N59 between Nancy and Colmar crosses the Vosges at Col du Bonhomme, from where roads lead to all places mentioned in the walks.

Area map: I.G.N. Carte Topographique, sheet 31.

The Vosges is a range of mountains bordering the Alsace plain and the Rhine valley in eastern France. Similar in character to the Black Forest on the Rhine's east bank, the Vosges mountains extend some 170km north to south, and are 20km wide in places. To the north, the range falls gradually away; the highest summits appear in the south and culminate in Le Grand Ballon (1,423m).

Although of respectable height, many Vosges hills are rounded and densely wooded with beech, pine and other species, only the loftiest tops being free of tree cover. Slopes are often gentle, but some — the result of glaciation — can be much steeper, providing spectacular views and frequently cradling a lake at their foot. Wildlife abounds, though not always at busy beauty spots: wild boar, foxes and deer are indigenous and chamois are thriving since their introduction in 1956.

Summer walking and winter skiing are both popular activities for the inhabitants of nearby towns such as Strasbourg, Colmar and Mulhouse. Visitors from further afield add to their numbers, especially at weekends. To cater for this influx, hotels, inns, ski-tows and other tourist amenities are being developed and the region is criss-crossed by many roads giving good access, as well as several scenic drives. Best known are the Route des Crêtes from Thann in the south to the Col du Bonhomme, threading the wooded crest on the old border between France and Germany; and the Route du Vin from Thann (west of Mulhouse) to Marlenheim (west of Strasbourg), connecting pretty villages and vineyards, many of great repute among connoisseurs.

Despite the area's popularity, it is easy to get off the beaten track and the main rambling organisation — Club Vosgien — has waymarked a large number of excellent walks, some short, others long-distance.

As in much hill country, the weather is changeable. Summer heat-haze can obscure clear views from the main summits down across the Alsace plain with its chequerboard fields and compact settlements. Equally, summer storms may be surprisingly heavy, while at other times mist and wind can keep conditions deceptively chilly.

When the weather is inclement, however, there are numerous delightful towns and villages to explore, rich in history and renowned for their Alsatian hospitality.

Perhaps the best time of year to visit the Vosges is in spring, when wild flowers are out and snow patches still linger on high north-facing slopes; or in autumn, when the woodlands are charged with colour. Both seasons see fewer visitors than the mid-summer and mid-winter peaks. There are two major towns beneath the southern Vosges' eastern slopes — Mulhouse and Colmar. For the holiday visitor, Mulhouse holds fewer attractions, being largely industrial. However, there is a very fine zoo in a 50-acre park, an imposing Renaissance Hôtel de Ville, a good

THE MAIN SIGHTS TO SEE IN STRASBOURG

•Thirteenth-century red sandstone Notre-Dame Cathedral, one of the noblest achievements of Western architecture: see the west front, medieval carvings of the Coronation and Death of the Virgin in the south doorway; the beautiful interior with magnificent stained glass; the 'Pillar of Angels' and the Astronomical Clock.

• Nearby stands 'Maison Kammerzell', the finest half-timbered house in Strasbourg.

• Numerous museums, including: Museum of Modern Art in the old Custom House; Municipal History Museum in the former Meat Market; Museums of Archaeology and Fine Arts in Château des Rohan; a Museum of Alsace.

•See the picturesque Tanners' Quarter in 'Little France', the old town surrounded by water.

• The modern Palais de l'Europe is the seat of the European Parliament.

• To the south and east of the city is the largest river port in France, at the confluence of the Rhine and Ill, and the Rhine-Marne and Rhine-Rhône canals; boat trips run round the docks.

•For all information on walking in the Vosges, contact ClubVosgien, 4 Rue de la Douane, 6700 Strasbourg.

• Main Office de Tourisme at 10 Place Gutenberg (Tel: 32 57 07).

WHAT TO SEE IN EPINAL

•This chief town of the Vosges department is surrounded by forest in the upper Moselle valley.

•The Vosges Museum contains medieval sculpture, paintings and 'Images d'Epinal' prints, for which the town is famous; visit 'Imagerie Pellerin' print works, 1km downstream on the right bank at 42 Quai de Dogneville.

• International Museum of Folk Art.

•A ruined château in a hill park.

•The fourteenth-century Basilica of St Maurice on the right bank.

•A covered market in an attractive arcaded square of sixteenth-century houses.

collection of paintings in the Musée des Beaux Arts as well as several museums, including one devoted to railways and another to textiles.

In considerable contrast, Colmar, capital of the department, has immense charm. Within the well-preserved old quarter there are carved half-timbered houses, narrow streets, fascinating shops and waterways in the picturesque 'Little Venice' crossed by old bridges. Many statues and fountains in the town are the work of the local nineteenth-century sculptor Bartholdi, creator of New York harbour's Statue of Liberty.

The celebrated Musée d'Unterlinden houses a collection of paintings, including the great Issenheim Altarpiece by Grünewald, folklore exhibits and local history, all housed in a thirteenth-century monastery which is also the venue for musical evenings each Thursday during the summer season. There is a Wine Fair in mid-August and a *Fête de la Choucroute* (sauerkraut) in September.

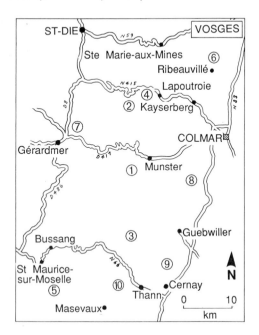

ROUTE 1: CIRCUIT OF LE HOHNECK AND PETIT HOHNECK

12km; 4hours. Total ascent about 400m. A climb in and out of forest to grassy summits and wide views.
   NOTE: Until the beginning of June, late-lying snow can be hazardous on north-facing slopes near the start of the walk.

Le Hohneck, second highest point in the Vosges, is one of the most interesting of all the tops. Its upper slopes are clear of tree cover, the environment there distinctly alpine in flavour, and many wild flowers can be found. Accessible by car up a rough track from the D430 Route des Crêtes, the summit of Le Hohneck is well visited and boasts a small café/hotel; until the turn of the century, this was the terminus of a mountain railway from Gérardmer.
   Lying east of the summits, Le Gaschney (993m) is well used to catering for visitors in all seasons and has hotel accommodation, restaurants and car parking. The town of Munster is a short drive away.
   Leave Le Gaschney to the right of a ski-lift, on a path climbing the north-east slopes of Le Petit Hohneck. Pass above the Schalleren hotel/restaurant, following blue triangular waymarks for Le Hohneck, and after having crossed

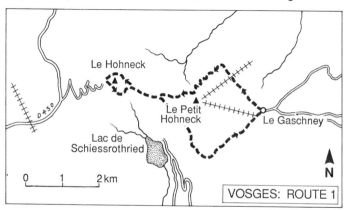

Near the summit of Le Hohneck

through meadows (ski-pistes in winter), enter forest. Level-
ling off for a stretch, the path provides marvellous views,
right, to the Martinswand cliffs across the Saint-Gregoire
valley.

Leave the forest and climb left up steeper, rough zigzags to another level — Col du Schaeferthal (1,230m). Le
Petit Hohneck is near at hand and can be reached easily
enough in clear weather. In mist it is best to follow waymarks
ahead (red rectangles — the yellow discs are ski-markers)
towards Le Hohneck itself.

Joining a broad ascending path, the café/hotel on Le
Hohneck soon slips into sight and easy slopes lead to
the   *table d'orientation* on the summit (1,363m), whence
there are wide panoramas over the wooded Vosges mountains.

NEARBY TOWNS OF INTEREST

Munster
•Start of the 'Route du Fromage', a town noted for its fine cheeses.

•See the 1555 Town Hall and 1503 Laub (Market Hall).

•A good centre for excursions.

Gérardmer
•Situated in an area containing many beautiful lakes, including Lac de Gérardmer, Lac de Longemer and Lac de Retournemer.

•A year-round resort with facilities for water and winter sports.

•Casino, numerous hotels, campsites.

•Office de Tourisme de Vosges at BP5, 88400 Gérardmer (Tel: (29) 63-08-74).

Facing back towards Le Petit Hohneck, follow the red rectangular waymarks to the right above the precipitous and impressive Wormspel valley, with magnificent views down to Lac de Schiessrothried in its glacial cirque.

After a bend left, leave the path heading back to Col du Schaeferthal and follow the grassy then stony track to the left of a chalet: here we are on the famous GR5 long-distance footpath from Holland to the Mediterranean, which traverses the Vosges before crossing the Alps on its way south.

Passing cliffs bearing many rock climbs, the track reaches Schiessroth farmstead, crosses a wooded ridge and enters pine forest. Finally, meadows lead easily back to Le Gaschney.

ROUTE 2: CIRCUIT OF LAC BLANC

4.5km; 2 hours. Total ascent about 225m. Lac Blanc occupies an extinct volcanic crater and the path climbs round beneath the crest of its wooded west and south edges, with spectacular views of the area.

NOTE: After rain, rocky sections of the path become very slippery.

From the car park at the Calvaire du Lac Blanc, an important crossroads south of Col du Bonhomme, take the broad, easy path south-west in pine forest, waymarked with red rectangles and signed 'Sentier des Trois Frontières' and 'Hautes Chaumes'. (This is also the GR5 long-

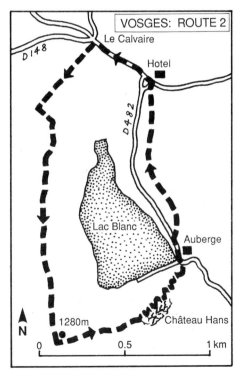

distance footpath, continuing along the ridge top parallel to this route.)

At a notice pointing out a view of the lake, leave the path on a track left, to join quickly another path south along the hillside (no waymarks). Ignoring all tracks which descend very steeply towards the lake, continue ahead with marvellous views left across the rugged crater. At the lake's southern end can be seen the 'Château Hans' rock tower, topped by a statue of the Virgin Mary.

Climbing gently, reach a spring of clear water (except in very dry summers) and the highest point of the walk — 1,280m. Following red-white-red paint flashes and signs for 'Digue du Lac Blanc' as far as the first pile of stones at the forest edge, take a path to the left, waymarked frequently with red rectangles. Descending steeply and provided with a handrail in places, the path joins a trod from the Rocher Hans and veers towards the dam now visible below. Beyond outcrops used for rock climbing, the going becomes less rocky and enters forest, zigzagging down to

Lac Blanc

SCENIC DRIVES IN THE SOUTHERN VOSGES

1) Route des Vosges —
from Klingenthal (near
Obernai, south-west of
Strasbourg) to Sélestat via
Mont Ste-Odile (a fascinat-
ing wooded ridge with a rich
and varied history of
occupation dating back to
Roman times), Hohwald and
Andlau.

2) Route des Crêtes —
75km of hilltop road con-
structed for strategic
purposes during World War I
and linking Col du
Bonhomme, Col de la
Schlucht, Le Markstein,
Grand Ballon, Vieil-Armand
War Cemetery and ending at
Mulhouse.

a car park and the Auberge de la Digue.

Cross the road and take a forest track (signed 'Orbey'
and waymarked with red-white-red paint flashes) for about
five minutes before forking left. A gentle slope leads past a
chalet and across meadow towards the Hôtel du Lac Blanc.
The road is followed back for a short distance to the Calvaire
car park.

Col de la Schlucht

ROUTE 3: CIRCUIT OF LE GRAND BALLON FROM COL DU HAAG

4.5km; 1¹/₂ hours. Total ascent about 185m. An easy climb
to the Vosges' highest summit, with wide-ranging panoramic views.

NOTE: Of little interest in mist! Although easily accessible from adjacent roads, this high top, bare of trees, is exposed to wind and weather; conditions can be deceptively chilly, even in summer. Le Grand Ballon is approx-
imately the same altitude as Ben Nevis, though lacking
Scotland's severe climate.

Col du Haag is situated on the scenic Route des Crêtes
(D431), north-west of Cernay. From the car park in front
of the Ferme-Auberge du Haag (1,240m — open as soon
as the Route des Crêtes is clear of winter snow), leave
the road on a path right (red rectangles) towards the
southern flanks of Le Grand Ballon. It crosses meadows
and after about 200m veers right to start climbing in
earnest.

Passing a small stream outlet, the route winds up
through bushes and loose stones, providing increasingly
magnificent views over the Thur valley and the neighbouring Ballon d'Alsace (1,247m) to the west.

At an altitude of 1,424m, the summit plateau of Le Grand
Ballon is soon reached, either by joining a direct path from
the road, or continuing on our present, less strenuous
course which leads left round slopes to the top. There is a
large and conspicuous monument to the *Diables Bleus*
who defended this hill in World War I, a *table d'orientation*,
some aerials and meteorological equipment. In very clear
weather, it is possible to see the snowy Alps ranged along
the southern horizon, from Santis to Mont Blanc; panoramic posters and cards are on sale at the restaurant which
will soon be reached. In early historical times, a shrine to
the sun god stood on this summit

Red rectangular waymarks lead down past the still-visible

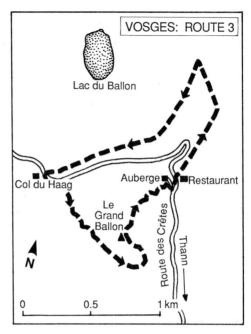

VOSGES: ROUTE 3

Lac du Ballon

Col du Haag   Auberge ■ ■ Restaurant

Le
Grand
Ballon

Route des Crêtes

Thann

N

0   0.5   1 km

remains of an ancient farm to the Hôtel du Grand Ballon and
across the D431 to the hexagonal 'Self-service Vue des
Alpes' restaurant — a very popular weekend destination for
visitors and locals alike.

On the left, our unwaymarked track proceeds clearly
along the ridge north-east. At a path signed 'Roedelen',
descend left over heather and reach a junction of two
broad tracks. Roedelen lies to the right, but our route
branches sharp left on the lower track, returning through
forest to the Route des Crêtes road and Col du Haag. The
lake glimpsed below, more clearly from higher up, is Lac
du Ballon, dammed in 1699 by the great French military
architect Vauban; today it is an industrial reservoir.

Just to the east, and built along the River Lauch at the
southern end of Alsatian wine-growing country, stands the
small town of Guebwiller. The terraces of vines were originally established by monks from the nearby abbey of
Murbach. Guebwiller's fine sixteenth-century Hôtel de Ville

NEARBY PLACES OF INTEREST

Le Markstein (1,176m)
•A saddle on the 'Route des Crêtes' above Lac de la Lauch. Good walking and winter skiing in the vicinity.

Guebwiller
•A delightful town on the River Lauch at the southern end of the Alsatian vine-yards, known as 'Florival', 'Valley of Flowers'.

•Eighteenth-century church of Notre-Dame with wood and stone carvings, also Romanesque church of St Léger.

•Sixteenth-century Town Hall.

•Museum and frescoes in the fourteenth-century former Dominican church; festivals of classical music there on the first Saturday of each month from June to September.

•The nearby Benedictine Abbey of Murbach and its twelfth-century church is one of the most important Romanesque buildings in Alsace, with original towers, transept and choir.

is worth seeing, as is its eighteenth-century church of Notre-Dame, rich with wood and stone carvings. On the first Saturday of the month from June to September, a festival of classical music is held in the now secularized fourteenth-century Dominican church, which also houses a museum.

Monument to
Les Diables Bleus

ROUTE 4: ETANG DU DEVIN
FROM LAPOUTROIE

13km   (plus 4km optional extension); $3^{1}/_{2}$-4 hours.   Total
ascent about 530m.   A circuit on good waymarked tracks
and lanes, in and out of forest up to a small lake. A further
optional climb leads to Tête des Faux, a strategic hilltop
during World War I and now an historic monument.

From the centre of Lapoutroie (car parking), take the road
which follows the Béhine river upstream (yellow disc waymarks). After about 2km, the road leaves Lapoutroie and
crosses the Béhine; but take a track left, still shadowing
the river on the edge of woods. At the next bridge, turn
sharp left up a track doubling back above the woods. Fork
right and watch for the same yellow waymarks as several
other lanes are crossed.

   Beyond the hamlet of Kébespre and a flatter stretch,
with good views over the Béhine valley, the route climbs
gradually, first near the edge of, then into forest, finally
winding up to emerge at a road and the small but impressive Etang du Devin, cradled beneath precipitous wooded
hillsides. The lake is marshy in places and surrounded by a
stony shoreline under the bulk of Tête des Faux.

   NOTE: For those with the necessary inclination and
energy, a further 350m of ascent leads up to the interesting summit of Tête des Faux. Follow the GR5 trail (red
rectangular waymarks) which leaves the lake's left (east)
shore, zigzagging steeply up through forest. Open ground
is gained at La Roche du Corbeau, 1,100m south-east of
Tête des Faux.

   These summits saw bitter fighting during World War I
and the remains of German fortifications are still in evi-
dence. A tunnel connected the two tops, while ammu-
nition and supplies were brought up by funicular railway
from Lapoutroie without risk to troops.

   From La Roche du Corbeau, GR5 drops to a ˌsaddle,
re-enters forest and zigzags up to Tête des Faux, with its

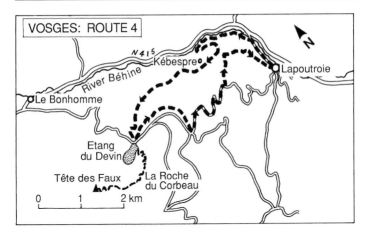

VOSGES: ROUTE 4

network of trenches, old bunkers and a large cross. From this elevation (1,220m), views are extensive and very beautiful in good conditions.

Return to Etang du Devin by the same route, allowing about 2 hours there and back.

From the north end of the lake, fork left off the road on a track adjacent to the ascent route and waymarked red-white-red. It drops pleasantly through woodland, emerging at a crossroads. Turn sharp left downhill (still waymarked) on the road's easy dog-legs. In just over 2km, a track leaves left towards the Béhine river, veering back right (south-east) into Lapoutroie village, avoiding a direct descent on the road.

Not far east from Lapoutroie, off the N475, stands the delightful town of Kayserberg. Apart from seeing the small museum dedicated to Albert Schweitzer who was born here, there is much to attract the visitor in this show-piece Alsatian settlement. Its ancient castle ruins overlook cobbled streets lined with geranium-decked medieval and sixteenth-century houses. Beneath steep-pitched roofs, shops sell a variety of local produce and artefacts, from wines and sausages to pottery and souvenirs. The main thoroughfare — Rue du Général de Gaulle — crosses a fifteenth-century fortified bridge bearing a small chapel, and passes a thirteenth to fifteenth-century church with an

WHAT TO SEE IN KAYSERBERG

•A popular wine town, once an important imperial city.

•Museum and birthplace of Albert Schweitzer (1875-1965).

•Picturesque fifteenth to seventeenth-century burghers' houses.

•The remains of medieval fortifications and castle ruins with keep, dismantled in 1632.

•Early Renaissance Town Hall and church of Ste-Croix.

•Interesting shops selling local ceramics; central fountain.

unusually interesting altarpiece and a fine Romanesque west front.

There are numerous hotels in Kayserberg and a nearby campsite: it would make an excellent centre from which to explore the southern Vosges.

Traditional costume in Kayserberg

ROUTE 5: BALLON D'ALSACE TO COL DES CROIX

$17^1/_2$km; $5^1/_2$-6 hours. A higher-level walk between two road cols, on good paths and forest tracks, involving some con-derable ups and downs, though the overall trend is a 500m loss of altitude. Superb viewpoints over neighbouring hills and valleys.

The N465 road runs in a series of sharp hairpin bends from Giromagny to Saint-Maurice-sur-Moselle, crossing the Col du Ballon close to the summit of Ballon d'Alsace, the southernmost top in the Vosges range. Both towns are well-provided with hotels, restaurants, shops, public trans-port and a campsite, and, for the keen walker, offer valley starting points for an ascent on foot to Ballon d'Alsace. From Giromagny, follow the GR5 waymarks (red and white) leaving from the east of the town — allow at least 4 hours for the 800m climb. From Saint-Maurice- sur-Moselle, take the Champs de la Faite et la Jumenterie track off the N465 south off the town, waymarked with red discs — allow about $2^1/_2$ hours for 600m of ascent.

This walk assumes a start from car parking on Col du Ballon (1,171m; inn and military museum) and a similar finish on Col des Croix (683m, hotel/restaurant).

To reach the summit of Ballon d'Alsace from Col du Ballon — a worthwhile detour — take the GR7 path north-east, passing a statue of Joan of Arc on horseback (dam-aged by lightning in 1973, reinstalled the following year). There are magnificent views over the Moselle valley. Curving south-east, the path attains the summit, with its Club Alpin Français viewing table and panoramas across the Vosges mountains, the deep Belfort valley and even to the Swiss Alps.

Five minutes away to the south-west stands a statue of the 'Vierge du Ballon', exactly on the old border between Alsace and France. There is a small restaurant nearby and walkers can proceed straight past this down to the road,

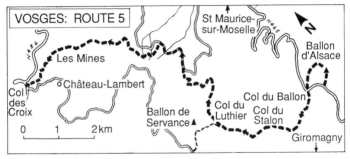

some 500m from the col, or return by the same route.

Cross the N465 and pass a monument to bomb disposal heroes of World War I. The route follows the long-
distance GR7 trans-Vosges footpath (concurrent for a time
with the GR59), waymarked in red and white. Through
beech forest, it proceeds past an old ski-ramp and drops
steeply to Col du Stalon (958m), on the watershed between the Rhône and the Rhine. At a junction here,
keep ahead on an ancient mule-track, climbing steadily
amongst trees, out over flowery pasture and past the
ruined Beurey farmstead to the shallow Col du Beurey
(1,130m).

The path now contours north-west for 1km to reach Col
du Luthier (1,100m), with good views ahead of the Ballon
de Servance's bare slopes and military buildings. A little way
beyond the col, the GR59 forks left down to the Saint-
Antoine forest and our route (still GR7) keeps right, over
a dry-stone wall by a ruin surrounded by scattered bushes
shaped by snow and wind.

A short climb leads to the final slopes below Ballon de
Servance, with more splendid views of the Presles gorges
and valley, La Jumenterie and the Ballon d'Alsace to the
east.

Losing height quickly in zigzags through forest, a
forestry track is soon reached, turning left and contouring
over stream beds, past a rough shelter to a junction. The
right fork drops into the Presles valley, so keep left to the
Bois du Hangy and across the Goute des Ordons torrent.
Leaving the main track (which joins a metalled road),

NEARBY PLACES OF
INTEREST

**Ballon d'Alsace
(1,250m)**
•Treeless summit plateau with
wide views.

•Statue of Virgin Mary and
monuments to Joan of Arc
and to the *Démineurs* (war-
time bomb disposal experts).

Bussang
•A mineral spring resort in
the upper Moselle valley on
the road to Col de Bussang
(733m).

•A monument at the source of
the River Moselle.

•Other nearby resorts of
interest include St Maurice-
sur-Moselle and Thillot.

climb to the Chalet de Longeligoutte, another basic shelter.
Turn left here on a broad track climbing to cross a stream
valley, then gently contouring for about 3.5km before
descending a stony road to Les Mines (685m).

Now an earth track leads to a tarred road, off which we
climb on a path to the left, passing a Calvary and entering
woods of pine and hazel beneath electricity cables. This
was an ancient thoroughfare before Col des Croix was
opened up. The statue of the Virgin Mary on the hilltop
ahead is a 1970 replacement for an 1855 original, de-
stroyed by lightning, erected to celebrate the sparing of the
local population from a cholera epidemic in 1854.

Less than 2km away lies Col des Croix, at which the walk
ends, but the nearby village of Château-Lambert is worth a
visit for its seventeenth-century church, and an ambience
unchanged in centuries.

ROUTE 6: A CIRCUIT OF THREE RIBEAUVILLE CHATEAUX

5km; 2 hours (excluding looking round the castles). A short but hilly walk, mostly in forest, to visit some notable châteaux. 362m of ascent involved.

This route connects three fine ruined châteaux: Haut-Ribeaupierre,Saint-Ulrich and Giersberg. The first and highest is situated on a hill top, the others about 100m below on a rocky hillside. Saint-Ulrich château owes its name to the chapel dedicated to this saint — of the three, it is the largest and best-preserved, the Ribeaupierre family having lived there for many years. In all Alsace, it is reckoned to be second only to the Haut-Koenigsbourg château as an outstanding example of feudal architecture and its tall, square keep, its chapel and the knights' quarters are well worth seeing.

Start from the parking area next to Ribeauvillé's sports ground at the top of Rue de Lutzelbach (280m) in the upper town. Passing in front of the sports ground, take a path on the right marked 'Châteaux par chemin ombrage' (shady path) and waymarked with a yellow cross. Continue ahead, alongside an orchard, at the end of which the track divides.Keep left here, more steeply uphill, and after crossing a forestry road, follow the sign 'Taennchel Thannenkirch Châteaux'.

Cross another forestry road and continue climbing on a path marked 'Haut-Ribeaupierre' and waymarked with red-white-red rectangles — taking care not to descend to Thannenkirch to the right. A sign indicates the 'Source du Chevreuil' spring near the path.

Access to Haut-Ribeaupierre château, at 642km is by either the north or south flanks. Visitors can climb to the top of the keep for a spectacular view across the Alsace plain.

Returning to the main entrance, take a path marked 'Ribeauvillé' and waymarked with red rectangles which winds down fairly steeply into forest. There are magnificent

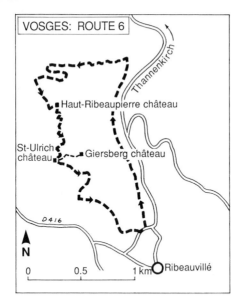

VOSGES: ROUTE 6

Thannenkirch

Haut-Ribeaupierre château

St-Ulrich château

Giersberg château

D 416

N

0   0.5   1 km Ribeauvillé

views, left, of the ruined Giersberg château to which the
route also leads.

In a short time, Saint-Ulrich château is reached, at 530m,
and a visit is strongly recommended, both for its architectural interest and for outstanding views. Allow at least an
hour. Before returning to Ribeauvillé, visitors with an imagin-
ative sense of history will find a short detour to Giersberg
château hard to resist. Perched on steep rocks at 528m, it
is the least well-preserved of the three, but an evocative
structure nonetheless. To reach it, follow a path marked
'Giersberg', with yellow crosses, allowing about 10 minutes
each way.

From Saint-Ulrich château, the descent to Ribeauvillé is
waymarked with red rectangles, weaving entertainingly
down a kind of botanical nature trail. At the exit of the
forest, a retrospective view reveals Saint-Ulrich château
etched imposingly against the sky. The walk ends by crossing a vineyard back to the starting point at the sports
ground.

WHAT TO SEE IN RIBEAUVILLE

•Delightful town and holiday resort, renowned for its nesting storks and its Reisling and Traminer wines. On the 'Route du Vin' surrounded by 400 hectares of vineyards.

•Half-timbered houses, a Renaissance fountain and a late Gothic monastic church.

•A wine market in July.

•The old town walls and towers, including the notorious 'Butchers' Tower'.

•Three magnificent ruined castles dating back to the eleventh and fourteenth centuries.

•A Strolling Musicians' Day on the first Sunday in September, with procession and folk celebrations.

St-Ulrich château ruins, Ribeauvillé

ROUTE 7: LA ROCHE DES BRUYÈRES

6km; 2 hours. A scenic, circular walk taking in a waterfall and some marvellous viewpoints in pleasant wooded hills. One steep section and an overall ascent of 256m.

The start is a car park opposite the Saut des Cuves hotel (700m) at the junction of the D417 Gérardmer to Col de la Schlucht, and the D8 to Saint-Dié. There are eating places nearby.

The route begins with a short circular loop to visit the Saut des Cuves. Take the main road east (towards Col de la Schlucht) for a few hundred metres, then cross the splendid stone bridge — Pont d'Amour — spanning the River Vologne on the right. Proceed along the river's left bank, passing attractive waterfalls, before crossing a metal bridge back to the car park.

Now take a shady track west, alongside the Vologne,

Winter in the Vosges, near Gérardmer

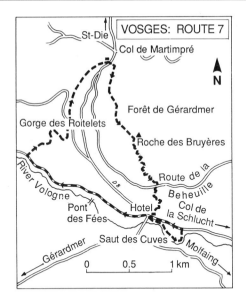

passing the Pont des Fées (Fairy Bridge) which dates from 1763, and continuing downstream. Tiny islands in the river — the Iles Marie-Louise — are reached over picturesque stone bridges.

In about 500m, the route approaches a dam, a short distance before which is a path climbing right and way-marked with red discs. It takes us up by a stream in the delightful Gorge des Roitelets, above a group of chalets and on to a metalled road which we follow left, still climbing.

Cross the road marked 'Molfaing' and look for a green rectangle and the sign 'Col de Martimpré'. Climbing gently, the path reaches the D8 road just before the col (where there is a restaurant) and veers sharp right into forest, now accompanied by red discs towards La Roche des Bruyères. Steep at first, the path emerges on to a forest track which is taken right, the gradient easing.

La Roche des Bruyères (906m) is signed to the right, and from this vantage point, Gérardmer and its surroundings are unfolded below in an outstanding view.

Returning to the main path and continuing south, we

WHAT TO SEE AT SAINT-DIE

•An attractive holiday town 30km to the north, extensively rebuilt after severe fire damage in 1944

•A fine fifteenth to sixteenth- century cathedral with beautiful cloisters.

•There are many kilometres of forest tracks and paths in the surrounding countryside.

---

reach a fork and keep right, waymarked with red discs and signed 'Saut des Cuves 2.5km'. The descent involves a series of steep zigzags. Arriving at a tarred road, turn right for 10m, then take a path below, well-marked, back to the car park.

ROUTE 8: NOTRE-DAME DU SCHAUENBERG AND OSENBUHR

8km; $2^1/_2$ hours. An undulating walk in and out of forest, past the Notre-Dame du Schauenberg pilgrimage chapel and the Osenbuhr settlement. Easy gradients, with a poss- ible short-cut if required.

The Schauenberg, a place of pilgrimage whose fifteenth- century chapel was restored in 1811, is a marvellous balcony viewpoint overlooking the Alsace vineyards, with a backdrop of the Black Forest and in the clearest weather the Alps themselves. A short detour is made to visit the charming hollow of Osenbuhr and a recommended ex- cursion would be to drive to Gueberschwihr, south of the start and one of the best-preserved medieval villages in the region.

There is a hotel/bar at Maison-Forestière Saint-Marc (438m), reached along the Gueberschwihr road from the N83 south of Colmar. From this village's main square, follow signs for Couvent Saint-Marc for 2.2km and leave the vehicle in the car park of the Maison-Forestière hotel.

Opposite, a large oak tree bears several signs, one reading 'Schauenberg' in a white rectangle. The track it denotes leads to a crossroad at the edge of forest, whence a well-waymarked path signed 'Schauenberg' is followed left, climbing gradually.

At 480m, we reach the so-called 'Kukuckstein', a rock shaped like a small table, and a bench nearby. Below lie vineyards and the magnificent Romanesque church at Gueberschwihr, built from pink sandstone.

The path now veers right and descends gently, passing blocks of rock and cliffs, with good views left. After crossing a parking area Notre-Dame du Schauenberg is reached, where there is an inn, a pilgrim's house and a chapel.

Our route is now signed 'Osenbuhr' and waymarked with red crosses to the left; ignore the forest track, right, which climbs the valley and which we eventually cross over.

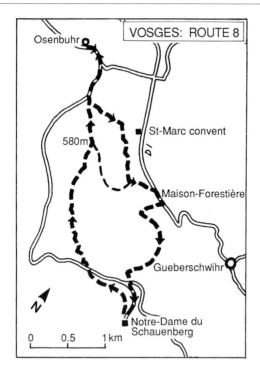

The pine forest here is a delight as we climb quickly to a more level stretch. Less important paths leave to the left, but stay on the main path with red cross waymarks.

Near the route's highest point at 580m, a path right returns to Maison-Forestière Saint-Marc in about 20 minutes if a short-cut is required. Continuing ahead, a resting point is not far away at Osenbuhr, soon glimpsed through foliage in a cleared area. A metalled lane leads to the inn and former convent, now a summer camp.

Retracing steps, watch for the path off left back towards the start, waymarked with red triangles then white rectangles. Saint-Marc convent and its surrounding pastures are visible through the trees on the left, and soon the forest is left behind as we cross two enclosed fields and take the road back to the car park.

PLACES OF INTEREST IN COLMAR

•Picturesque sixteenth and seventeenth-century burghers' houses in the old town.

•The Renaissance 'Maison des Têtes', covered with decorative heads and figures. Thirteenth-century Dominican church.

•The Unterlinden Museum, containing Grünewald's great Issenheim Altarpiece.

•An eighteenth-century Town Hall and several old churches.

•The sixteenth-century 'Maison Pfister', one of the best old houses in Colmar, with wooden galleries.

•The old Custom House.

•Charming little waterways and bridges in the 'Little Venice' quarter.

•St Martin's Cathedral.

•Statues and fountains throughout the town by local sculptor Bartholdi.

•Thursday evening summer musical evenings in the cloisters of the Unterlinden Museum.

•Various summer folk-lore events.

•A Wine Fair in mid-August.

•Office de Tourisme at 4 Rue d'Unterlinden (Tel: 41 02 29).

A street in Colmar

ROUTE 9: A TOUR OF THE VIEIL-ARMAND WORLD WAR I MILITARY MEMORIAL SITE

5km; 2hours (excluding halts). A circular walk past World War I fortifications, ruined buildings and French and German memorials. One or two steep sections, but well-waymarked. Good views.

The Vieil-Armand, or Hartmannwillerkopf, poses many questions as to the morality of war and the values of our civilisation: over 60,000 men in the prime of life died on the surrounding hillsides and in the trenches, the remains of which will be encountered.

Follow the D431 road linking Markstein with Uffholtz Cernay, via Col Amic, and leave the vehicle at Le Silberloch car parking, altitude 908m. Refreshments are available here.

Enter the cemetery, passing in front of the Autel and Patrie memorial above the crypt (exhibition), and descend along the central path to Col du Silberloch where there is a battlefield plan. Proceed ahead, following red crosses and red-white-red waymarks, to reach the French positions and the concrete *Croix Sommitale*. The route now descends towards the *Diables Rouges* (French) and the *Chasseurs Bavarois* (German) monuments.

Our path is now waymarked with blue rectangles and passes in front of an old army outpost before leading on to a network of trenches and German structures. A large iron cross surmounts the main German fortification, from which superb viewpoint the Alps are visible in clear weather.

Follow a path opposite, red cross waymarks, leading to the right as far as the *Diables Rouges du 152 R.I.* monument, erected against the rock on the Rehfelsen fortress and German cableway station. From here, drop to the signpost below and take a path marked 'Wuhnheim' (red-white-red rectangles) descending quite steeply in zigzags. Past the cableway station and fallen rocks, a former German military road is reached — Voie Serpentine — which is

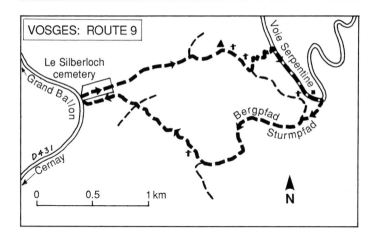

VOSGES: ROUTE 9

Le Silberloch cemetery

Grand Ballon

Voie Serpentine

D431 Cernay

Bergpfad

Sturmpfad

0   0.5   1 km

N

followed to the right. At a hairpin bend shortly after a ruined depot, take a narrow path right, signed 'Sturmpfad' which soon emerges on the Bergpfad path towards the *Serret* monument.

(Five minutes away to the right stands the imposing *Chasseurs* monument, a rocky plinth bearing plaques dedicated to the famous German units. It is a magnificent viewpoint over the Alsace plain.)

Following yellow discs as well as red-white-red rect-angles, the level path contours round hillside with good views over Cernay and the Thur valley. Several fortified pos-itions of exceptional interest are passed.

Once over the French trenches, a path junction is reached. Leave the red-white-red waymarks and ascend to the right alongside a stream. The *Serret* monument soon appears on the left, in memory of the French General Serret, killed during combat in 1915. The climb is fairly steep until the stream and a forestry road are crossed, after which the cemetery is skirted, left, and steps descended to the car park.

*The Vieil-Armand
World War I
military cemetery*

NEARBY PLACES OF INTEREST

•The Vieil-Armand or Hartmannwillerkopf Military Cemetery. On the 'Route des Crêtes' from Col du Bonhomme to Mulhouse.

•World War I cemetery for 60,000 men on the site of bitter combat.The crypt contains the remains of 12,000 unknown soldiers.

•A French memorial cross and monuments.

•Old German positions still visible.

•Waymarked paths and a small restaurant.

ROUTE 10: THE THANNERHUBEL AND COL DU ROSSBERG FROM COL DU HUNDSRUCK

7km; 2$^{1}/_{2}$ hours. A circuit of a Vosges summit, in and out of forest past mountain inns and pasture, with exceptional views. Some 400m of ascent but nowhere steep. Much of this walk is in pleasant tree shade and the Thannerhubel viewpoint is reputed to be one of the finest in the Vosges region.

Start from car parking on Col du Hundsruck, on the Route Joffre D14 between Masevaux and Bitschwiller-les-Thann. Refreshments are available at Col du Hundsruck and Thannerhubel.

From the col, altitude 746m, in front of La Fourmi restaurant, a road drops towards Willer-sur-Thann on the north-east flank of the Thannerhubel mountain. Just above this junction, take a path signed 'Thannerhubel' and way-marked with red rectangles. It leads through forest and out across pasture at Haut-de-Bourbach.

Where paths fork, keep right on a stony surface, now following red triangles, and climb gently through beautiful pine forest, over one forestry track and joining another. Leaving the trees, there is a magnificent view ahead of the Thannerhubel summit, and to the right the Thann valley dominated by the Grand-Ballon. Pass above the Thanner-hubel farm-inn and climb on, following blue triangles, towards the Club Vosgien refuge which is passed to the left. As altitude is gained, views open out over the Vosges range.

Contouring round the Thannerhubel's northern slopes, the path enters and leaves a beech wood before dropping gently to pastures and the Ferme Moyenne du Rossberg. From here, a path signed 'Rossberg' and waymarked with red rectangles ascends south to Col du Rossberg (1,120m), situated between the Thannerhubel and Ross-berg tops.

(A possible extension to the walk leaves west from here

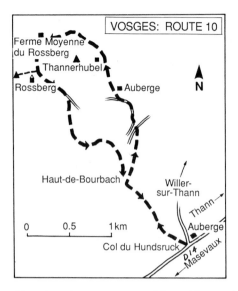

along the Rossberg's stony, scrubby ridge, giving airy views which are extensive and exciting from the rocky summit at 1,180m. Allow about half an hour each way.)

The Rossberg Ski-Club refuge stands right on the col

Domestic architecture in Alsace

TOWNS OF INTEREST NEARBY

Thann
•An industrial town at the mouth of the Thur valley and at the southern end of the 'Route du Vin'.

•Remains of the seventeenth-century Englebourg Castle, with Witches, Storks and Flea towers.

•Arcaded market place and part-medieval Town Hall.

•St Thiébaut church, a fine Gothic structure reminiscent of Strasbourg Cathedral, with a graceful 76m high tower, magnificent doorways; the interior contains beautiful carvings and stained glass.

•Half-timbered houses and several fountains.

•A Museum of Alsatian History in the sixteenth-century Cornmarket (Halle aux Blés).

Masevaux
•A health resort in the Doller valley.

•Sixteenth and seventeenth-century burghers' houses and an eighteenth-century fountain.

•Above the town stands the Rossberg (1,191m), with easy ascent paths.

•A scenic road leads up the Doller valley to Lac d'Alfeld and the Ballon d'Alsace; there is also a 14km 'train touristique' line along the Doller valley from Cernay.

Long-distance paths
(ending at Masevaux and waymarked by local clubs)
Wissembourg to Masevaux — 388km (red rectangles)
Lembach to Masevaux — 282km (blue rectangles)
Obersteinbach to Masevaux — 324km (yellow rectangles)

There are also many linking paths from railway stations and villages, all waymarked with red and white stripes.

and a sign on a tree ahead indicates our route along a broad track, slowly dropping towards forest. There is a good view here over the Masevaux valley. In about ten minutes, a path signed 'Hundsruck' forks right and leads back to the start

2 The Ardennes

How to get there

Nearest airports: Paris (Charles-de-Gaulle), Lille, Brussels and Luxembourg.

Rail: Good rail links from Paris (Gare-de-l'Est) and channel ports to Charleville-Mézières and Sedan.

Road: A26 and N43 from channel ports to Charleville-Mézières; or A4 and N51 from Paris.

Area map: I.G.N. Carte Topographique, sheet 5.

The Ardennes is a region in the old province of Champagne, near France's border with Belgium. Although much of Champagne-Ardennes is a chalky plain, well-suited to vineyards, the most northerly parts are heavily wooded and offer much to the visitor who is prepared to walk on some of the many footpaths there.

The Ardennes region is sometimes called *pays de forêt* and is, indeed, a richly-forested country, dissected by steep valleys and dramatic rocks and scattered with old fortresses and châteaux. The hills, clothed by woodland, are not particularly high, rising to around 500m, but contain many kilometres of good walking trails, in addition to canal and river towpaths.

Deer and wild boar live in the forests, but are preserved for sport and are unlikely to be seen by the passing visitor. This is hunting country, with game and fish featuring prominently on local menus. Although champagne should be tasted at least once in this its home department, Ardennes beer is also very good.

The River Meuse flows in great serpentine swings through this area, passing two of the major towns, Sedan and Charleville-Mézières. Further north it penetrates close-ly-wooded slopes towards Givet and the Belgian frontier.

Sedan, an ancient citadel town on a bend in the Meuse not far from Luxembourg, is today rather industrialised, dilut-ing its many historical associations. In 1870 it was the scene of Napoleon III's surrender to the Prussians which led to the subsequent siege and capitulation of Paris — a disastrous defeat for France. And the town figured in both World Wars, suffering severe damage in World War II. Sedan's great attraction is its massive fortified château, one of the largest in Europe and dating from the fifteenth century. Its 30m-high ramparts provide excellent view-points over the town and surrounding countryside, and as well as moats and bastions, the interior houses an histor-ical museum.

Until 1966, Charleville-Mézières — the other large centre — was two separate towns. Mézières is the older part, a medieval walled enclave on the south bank of the Meuse, with a splendid Basilica Notre-Dame wherein Charles IX married Elizabeth of Austria in 1570. Charleville, to the north, was established in 1606 and provides an interesting example of seventeenth-century gridiron town planning, with its elegant Ducal Square an imposing feature, es-pecially on market days. The poet Rimbaud was born in Rue Thiers, and there is a very good Museum of the Ardennes in the Vieux Moulin by the River Meuse to the north of the town. Like Sedan, Charleville-Mézières was badly damaged during World War II. Either of these towns would make an excellent centre for exploring the Ardennes by car and on foot.

Being far enough east to avoid most of the Atlantic weather systems, the Ardennes enjoys a climate percep-tibly drier than more westerly parts of northern France. Summers tend to be warmer, winters chillier. Spring and

WHAT TO SEE IN CHARLEVILLE-MEZIERES AND SEDAN

Charleville-Mézières
•Originally two settlements, Mézières is the older walled town on the River Meuse's south bank. Its Notre-Dame Basilica is well worth visiting.

•Charleville, to the north, is arranged on a seventeenth-century grid pattern.

•Ducal Square is particularly impressive, especially on market days.

•Birthplace of the poet Rimbaud is in Rue Thiers; a Museum of the Ardennes in the Vieux Moulin by the river.

•Office de Tourisme — 2 Rue Mantoue (Tel: 33 00 17).

Sedan
•Situated towards the border with Luxembourg on a big bend in the River Meuse.

•Visit the massively fortified fifteenth-century château — it is one of Europe's biggest, with 30m-high ramparts, moat and bastions.

•There are excellent town views from the walls and an Historical Museum inside.

•The town also has a monument to Maréchal Turenne (1611-75).

THE MEUSE VALLEY

•The River Meuse is closely followed north by the N51 through Revin and Givet to the Belgian border. There is glorious river and forest scenery, with several old forts and châteaux.

•Impressive rocky outcrops and cliffs include: Rochers des Grands Ducs, north of Nouzonville; Rochers des Dames de Meuse, north of Monthermé and visible from the road; Roche des Quatre Fils Aymon, Roche aux Sept Villages and Roche de Roma, all south of Monthermé; Roche de la Faligeotte near Revin; Roche de l'Uf and Rocher à Fépin near Haybes. Many accessible by footpath.

•15km north-west of Charleville-Mézières lies Lac des Vieilles Forges, a beautiful lake surrounded by woodland, with amenities for swimming and sailing. There are many kilometres of towpath walking south of Sedan along the Canal des Ardennes. Water sports and bathing are enjoyed on Etang de Bairon.

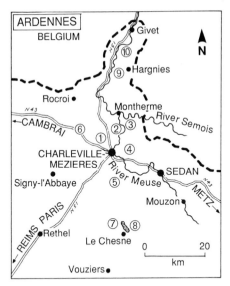

autumn often bring long dry spells, ideal for walking; autumn is perhaps the best time of all, with crisp, clear air and stunning colours as tree foliage turns with the first frosts.

The following walks are mostly around 15km (about 9 miles) in length, a few longer. Gradients are generally moderate and steeper sections short-lived — no great height gain is involved on any walk. Stout footwear is strongly advised, both for cushioning on hard tracks and country roads, and for grip on forest paths which can be muddy in wet weather. A spare sweater and energy rations in the form of chocolate or sweets are useful items to have in reserve, while on the longer routes, a pre-packed meal might be carried. Many villages have a bar or shop, but not the smaller hamlets. All the walks are circular and many can be cut short if time or condtions are pressing.

ROUTE 1: AROUND CHARLEVILLE-MEZIERES AND WOODS TO THE NORTH

14km; 4 hours. A circuit from the old town of Charleville-Mézières, up through woods alongside the lovely River Meuse and ending in attractive public gardens.

The walk starts at the Vieux-Moulin (Old Mill, which also houses a Museum of the Ardennes), to the north of the town, where the River Meuse describes a big loop before flowing north in its densely wooded valley. Follow the Rimbaud quayside and continue along by the Meuse to Sous les Roches ('Under-Rocks'). Just before a tall building, go left on a path which meets the D1 road. Pass in front of the Bel-Air psychiatric hospital and at the next crossroads take the Culbute housing estate road.

The route first passes alongside La Havetière woods, then enters them, crossing a stream and taking an uphill

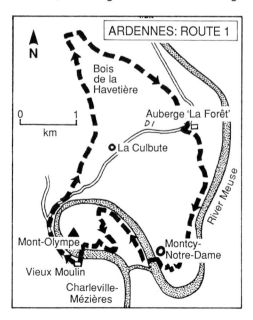

Place Ducale in Charleville

track. After about 2km and before a clearing is reached,
turn right. Walk beneath some electricity cables and, turning south-east now, meet a track along the ridge above
Nouzonville. Descend to L'Auberge 'La Forêt', cross over
the D1, then take a small unsurfaced lane from Montcy-
Notre-Dame in front of the inn. Near a warehouse, turn
left on a track through woods, pass back under the electricity cables and emerge near Montcy-Notre-Dame's
cemetery.

Go through the village and cross the River Meuse near
the church. Turn right immediately and keep by the river
into Montcy-St-Pierre, continuing on to reach the attractive
Mont-Olympe area in the river loop. Return to the start is
made via the public gardens and footbridge.

ROUTE 2: MEILLIER-FONTAINE AND JOIGNY-SUR-MEUSE FROM NOUZONVILLE

13km; 4 hours. A circular walk, climbing through woods and dropping to the River Meuse, connecting Nouzonville with two picturesque villages.

Start on the west bank of the Meuse by the Nouzonville bridge, and take a minor road west which leaves to the right of a petrol station. This climbs to Devant-Nouzon in the Seigneurs woods and becomes a path which meets the Nouzonville to Meillier-Fontaine road. At Meillier village, clustered on its little hill around the church, follow the red and white paint flashes of the GR12 long-distance foot-path from Ile-de-France to the Ardennes. These lead on,

By the River Meuse

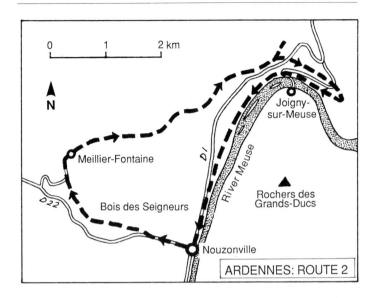

0   1   2 km

N

Joigny-
sur-Meuse

Meillier-Fontaine

D1

River Meuse

D22

Bois des Seigneurs

Rochers des
Grands-Ducs

Nouzonville

ARDENNES: ROUTE 2

past the cemetery and on to a forestry track, dropping gently. Before the track descends finally towards Bogny-sur-Meuse, turn right on the waymarked path, cross the D1 road and meet the Bogny to Joigny road.

Continue to the footbridge at Joigny and, as this is crossed, there are very good views of the Rochers des Grands-Ducs to the south. These rocky outcrops, though not the most outstanding in the region, are one of many such features formed by the Meuse on its tortuous course.

From the footbridge, a path straightforwardly follows the west bank of the Meuse back to Nouzonville.

ROUTE 3: THE ROCHES DES QUATRE FILS AYMON, FROM TOURNAVAUX

11km; 3-4 hours. A climb to a well-known local beauty spot with rock outcrops and exceptional views. Return alongside the River Semois.

The River Semois meanders west to join the Meuse at Monthermé and between the two rivers before they meet stands a shapely wooded hill with a series of rock out-crops, known as the Quatre Fils Aymon, focal point for this route.

Start at the Tournavaux bridge, on the west bank of the River Semois, and follow the road towards Phade for about 200m, thereafter taking a sharp left turn on an uphill path by the Relorse stream. The ridge (though not the sum-mit itself) is reached at 299m and, at a junction, take a path right, then almost immediately a straight track left in the direction of La Roche-Bayard (south-west). White way-

The Meuse at Monthermé

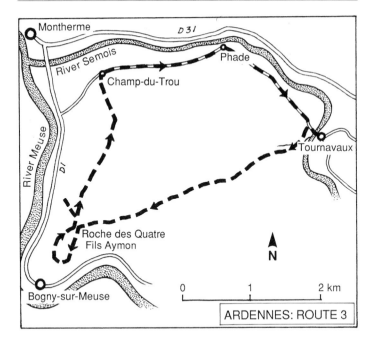

ARDENNES: ROUTE 3

marks guide visitors round a circuit of the Roches des
Quatre Fils Aymon, with exceptional views over the Meuse
valley. The four quartzite outcrops are said to resemble, in
silhouette, horsemen from a French legend.

Returning from the circuit, take a path passing the end
of an ancient cart-track, following it to its end and continuing beyond on a descending track to Champ-du-Trou.
The minor road to Phade now leads pleasantly along the
Semois, back to the start at Tournavaux.

(**NOTE**: Nearby Monthermé, set in a dramatic, steep-
sided bend at the confluence of the Meuse and Semois, is
well worth visiting. It is surrounded by rocky crests such as
the one just explored, and by much delightful woodland.
Large sixteenth-century frescoes in the fortified St Leger
church have been carefully restored.)

ROUTE 4: AIGLEMONT, LA GRANDVILLE AND GESPUNSART

18km; 5¹/₂-6 hours. A longer, undulating walk, partly in delightful forest on tracks and woodland paths, over stream valleys and visiting an attractive village.

Start on the D58 road about 1km north of Aiglemont at Croix-Baudet. A path leads down right and in 1¹/₂km arrives at the D57 road, which we follow, right, for only 10m, immediately turning left and climbing to the forestry road between Gespunsart and La Grandville. Follow this south as far as the N379 road and walk up this for a kilometre or so to the beginning of La Grandville.

Take the first alleyway left, then walk down a street almost opposite, which becomes a forest road and eventually a very lovely woodland path, dropping over the valley of La Vrigne and meeting another forest road. Turn up left

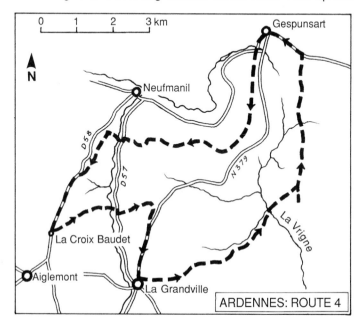

ARDENNES: ROUTE 4

Notre-Dame-de-l'Espérance, Mézières

here and contour along below the Bois Communaux to Gespunsart.

Continue through the village and turn left on the forest road to La Grandville, staying on it for $2^1/_2$km. Before the second bend, take a short stretch of sunken path, then turn right on another delightful way through forest and down to the D57 road. Cross a waste tip and the Trois-Fontaines stream and, after climbing again to the ridge, watch for an attractive path left, leading to the 'Petit Sabot' and the D58 back to La Croix Baudet.

(**NOTE**: walkers continuing ahead from the ridge, over the D58 and up the Fontaine-de-Gravis stream may find paths obscured or changed due to new afforestation.)

ROUTE 5: VILLERS-SUR-LE-MONT AND SINGLY, FROM BALAIVES-ET-BUTZ

15km; 4-5 hours. A circuit through undulating countryside, partly wooded, on good tracks and country roads through two villages.

Leave Balaives-et-Butz, in its valley setting, by climbing from the 'Place' (sportsground) westwards to the edge of forest. Here, bear left on a pleasant track as far as the D233 road at La Gross-Borne.

(**NOTE:** about half way along at the hill top, the track is rather overgrown.) Cross the D233 and continue ahead, south, along the edge of the Forêt d'Elan. At the corner of forest, turn 90° right on an earth track for about 1½km to reach the village of Singly.

The walk now proceeds along the Villers-sur-le-Mont country road, north-west from the village centre. At Villers,

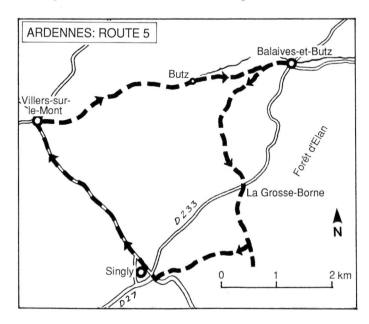

ARDENNES: ROUTE 5

Balaives-et-Butz

Butz

Villers-sur-le-Mont

Forêt d'Elan

La Grosse-Borne

D233

N

Singly

D27

0   1   2 km

Sedan's mighty château

turn right on a delightful track down to Butz, returning to
Balaives on a path alongside the Ruisseau de Butz, past
Flamanville farm over on the left.

ROUTE 6: REMILLY-LES-POTHEES TO WARBY AND RETURN VIA THE FORET DU HAILLY AND NEUFMAISON

17km; about 5 hours. A walk through typical Ardennes countryside and forest, on good tracks and lanes and passing through two villages in the River Thin valley.

Though a little longer than most in this region, the walk is easy to follow. Leave Remilly on a very attractive path west of the castle, walking south-east and keeping ahead at various turnings-off around Croix-Jean. The way winds and undulates, passing beneath electricity cables, before drop-

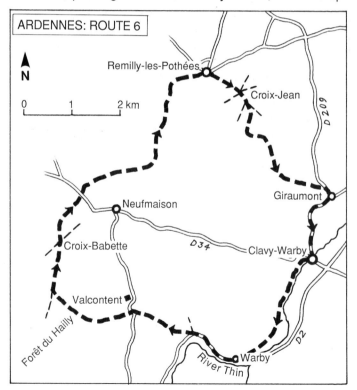

ping east to the D209 road just before the small village of
Giraumont. Keep right, opposite the church, and in 1km
arrive at Clavy-Warby on the Ruisseau de Thin. Here we
pick up the GR12 long-distance trail for a while (it connects
Ile-de-France with the Ardennes), following its red and
white painted waymarks.

The route keeps to the west bank of the Thin below
woods, and reaches Warby hamlet, whence the GR12
continues south. We now walk west, however, on the D2
country road for 1km, then turn right on to a path at a
Calvary just as the road and river bend left. Keep left at a
lane (a short-cut, if required, to Neufmaison), past Val-
content farmstead, then turn right in about $1^1/_2$km and
follow the path north to Croix-Babette.

Keep ahead, passing close to Neufmaison on the right,
go over the D34 road and walk back on a good track to
Remilly-les- Pothées.

ROUTE 7: CIRCUIT 'A' FROM ETANG DE BAIRON ALONG THE CANAL DES ARDENNES

15km; 4-5 hours. Lakeside, woodland and canal walking past locks, interspersed with farmland. (Sailing and bathing in the lake.)

From the west end of Bairon village, cross the N991 road and take a path west, then down left to reach the D30 road, along which turn right, past L'Orphane farmstead to Longwé. The road makes a big hairpin bend over the valley of the Ruisseau de Longwé, but we climb left before this, up the Montardré track and down to the Canal des Ardennes at lock (*écluse*) no 10.

Turn left along the canal towpath and continue to lock no 1. Keep straight on here, still on the towpath for just over 2km, when Le Chesne is reached. At the far end of the village, on the road towards Sedan (N77), take a track left alongside the Louis- Page sports ground; this leads up and over to the Etang de Bairon. Cross a footbridge and follow the west bank of the lake up to Bairon.

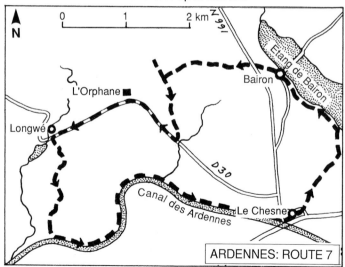

ARDENNES: ROUTE 7

ROUTE 8: CIRCUIT 'B' FROM ETANG DE BAIRON, ALONG THE CANAL DES ARDENNES

14km; 4-4¹/₂ hours. Lakeside and canal towpath walking, connected by undulating countryside and farmsteads. (Sailing and bathing in the lake.)

Cross the central dam separating the older northern section of the lake from the newer southern extension, turning left along the north bank. The path leads up to Les Courtiseaux farm, whereupon we turn left, climbing to the ridge and emerging at the D8 road which is followed, right, to Sauville village. Here, walk along the D12 towards Vendresse and at the edge of woods, take a track right, to La Gravelle farm. A continuation of this leads down to the Canal des Ardennes.

Turn right along the towpath and about 800m beyond a bridge over the canal, turn right. This path through trees crosses both the D8 and D12 roads and leads to La Baronnerie farm, proceeding ahead past the campsite at St Brice and back to Bairon.

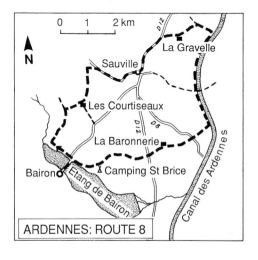

ARDENNES: ROUTE 8

ROUTE 9: THE FEPIN ROCK, CHATEAU DU RIDOUX AND THE OLD LIMBOURG MILL FROM HARGNIES

16km; 4-5 hours. A circular walk, much of it in forest but with good views over the River Meuse. Riverside towpath, a château, a stream valley and an old mill lead back to the starting village.

The walk begins at Hargnies, taking the D7 road south-west towards Haybes. At a sharp left bend by the Auberge du Cousin (inn), turn off right on a path in woods, signed 'Roches de Fépin'. As the path descends towards the River Meuse, a short detour left is possible to see the rocks. There are good views for most of the way and at the river, turn right along the towpath towards Château du Ridoux (or Risdoux). Turn right up between the château itself and some out-buildings on a delightful track following the Ridoux stream.

At a junction in a clearing replanted with conifers, cross a feeder stream and climb steeply right, the gradient soon easing back. Passing the old Limbourg mill, the route keeps right and follows the track back up to Hargnies.

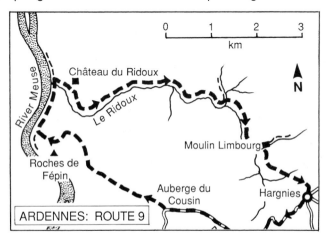

ROUTE 10: RANCENNES AND THE RIVER MEUSE, CHOOZ AND CHARNOIS VILLAGES

13km; 3¹/₂-4 hours. Country walking with river towpath, a clifftop viewpoint and a wooded climb, taking in three villages.

Start the walk from a small *oratoire* 500m north of Rancennes village. The route forks left (north) up a tarred lane, swinging round left to Aviette farm down by the River Meuse. The towpath is then followed for 2¹/₂km to Petit Chooz (Chooz can also be visited by crossing the bridge). We have arrived at a big loop in the River Meuse, its neck spanned by a navigable tunnel. A recommended 'extra' is to climb a rather steep path from near a house just before the bridge, to reach a very fine viewpoint atop the cliffs.

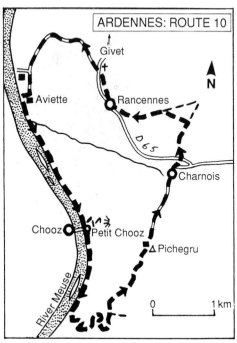

ARDENNES: ROUTE 10

The deeply-cut river bend and an impressive power station are seen to good effect from here.

Continue along the towpath and in just over 1km, leave it for a stony track left which zigzags uphill. Keep left until the ridge top is reached and turn left again near a trig point and Pichegru farm to arrive at Charnois. Go through the hamlet and keep in the same direction past the cemetery on a path for about 750m. Turn left and after 500m, left again, walking back to Rancennes.

(**NOTE**: Just to the north, the historic town of Givet stands astride the Meuse, dominated to the west by the massive Charlemont fortress built in 1555 and fortified by the great French military architect Vauban. Also in Givet are the Tour Victoire (fourteenth and fifteenth century) and Tour Grégoire on Mont-d'Haurs, a panoramic viewpoint.)

The River Meuse at Givet

3 The Forêt D'Orient and Pays D'Othé

How to get there

Nearest airports: Paris (Orly) and Nancy.

FORET D'ORIENT

Rail: Good connections to Troyes from Paris Gare-de-l'Est.

Road: N19 east from Paris.

Area map: I.G.N. Carte Topographique, sheet 22.

Champagne is a pleasant region of north-east France, its southern hillslopes providing that most light and aristocratic wine for which the area is renowned worldwide. Though no great distance from large bustling towns like Reims and Dijon, not to mention Paris itself, the undulating country-side, with its vineyards and valleys, presents a cheerful face to the visitor. Its very openness, however, undefended in all directions, gave rise to fierce fighting in three Franco-German wars and while the scars of battle have largely dis-appeared from the land, some remain as memorials and there are many military cemeteries.

Champagne-sèche — the chalky northern sector which produces champagne — leads south to Champagne-humide with its forests, lakes and stock-farms. This latter area, in the Aube department, offering woodland rambles, riding, fishing, water-sports and observing wildlife in natural habitats, is the focus of attention.

Lac du Der Chantecoq, near Saint-Dizier, stretches over 12,400 acres, France's largest man-made lake. However,

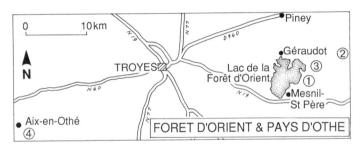

Lac de la Forêt d'Orient is the chosen centre. It is part of a
Regional Nature Conservation Park 30km to the south and
has a wildlife reserve, bird sanctuary, ancient forest and is
close to Troyes.

Troyes is a good base from which to explore the Aube.
Situated on the River Seine 150km south-east of Paris, it
has prospered since Gallo-Roman times, particularly during
the Middle Ages when many great fairs were held here.
Today it is chief town of the Aube and a traditional centre of
the hosiery trade.

Narrow streets of ancient gabled houses alternate with
modern shopping malls and open squares. The town pos-
sesses several fine ecclesiastical edifices, notably Ste
Madeleine, St Pantaléon and the thirteenth-century
basilica of St Urbain. But the cathedral of St Peter and St
Paul is the real highlight. Taking four centuries to build
(the second tower was never completed), it is a splendid
Gothic structure, richly endowed with carvings and beautiful stained glass. The 'Treasure' — marvellous enamels and
goldwork — is housed in a thirteenth-century vaulted hall.

Also well worth seeing is Troyes' Musée des Beaux Arts
in the former Bishop's Palace (*Ancien Evêché*) near the
cathedral — both for its architectural interest and its
exhibits, amongst which are fifteenth to twentieth-century
paintings and drawings, sculpture and African and Oriental
art; other sections represent local archaeology, natural
history, manuscripts and there is a large library.

Visitors will find a number of good hotels to choose from
in Troyes, while campsites are to be found in the surrounding countryside at such places as Estissac on the

N60, Romilly on the N19, Arcis on the N77 and at Géraudot
and Mesnil-St Père on the Lac de la Forêt d'Orient.

The Regional Nature Conservation Park of the Forêt
d'Orient, inaugurated in 1970, embodies a mysterious
period in French history, associated with the soldier-monks
of the *Ordre du Temple* and *Ordre des Chevaliers de la
Milice du Christ* — the Templiers — who served under
Napoleon. (There is a military school and Musée Napoléon
at Brienne-le-Château.)

The park, a large area 15km east of Troyes, consists
mainly of forest, rivers and stretches of water. Clayey soil
helps maintain the ancient Forêt du Der oaks which once
covered the entire region, whilst around its perimeter are
many copses, lakes and meadows in gently undulating
countryside, increasingly being given over to cereal crops

Extending over 5,700 acres, the Lac de la Forêt d'Orient
is part of a vast drainage control system constructed in
1965 to prevent flooding of the Seine and its tributaries,
with similar work in prospect for the River Aube. Old photographs in the Maison du Parc Forestry Centre graphically
portray the effects of flooding prior to these preventative
measures.

All forms of motorised craft are barred from using the lake,
and no portable radios etc may be played in the park.
Wildlife of all kinds is thus largely undisturbed and a peaceful environment is created for bird watching (within the
sanctuary, many species of duck, grebe and heron breed
in the shallow pools), sailing, fishing, bathing and walking.

FURTHER INFORMATION AND NEARBY PLACES OF INTEREST

Lac de la Forêt d'Orient and Lac du Der-Chantecoq

•Two lakes 30km apart, providing opportunities for sailing, bathing (sandy beaches), fishing, horse-riding, rambling on forest and lakeside trails, bird-watching.

•Wildlife Reserve at Lac de la Forêt d'Orient.

•*Motor Museum:* In modern, purpose-built setting at Villiers-en-Lieu, 4km north-west of Saint-Dizier.

•*Napoleonic Museum:* At Brienne-le-Château, just north of Lac de la Forêt d'Orient. Dedicated to Napoleon who spent 5 years at Military College here, from 1779 to 1784.

•Also at Brienne-le-Château is a splendid late-eighteenth-century château in parkland, and a timber-framed market hall.

Bar-sur-Aube

•A small, attractive market town near the Clairvaux Forest.

•Two very old churches, one of which, St Pierre, has unusual wooden balconies.

Troyes

•A town of Gallic and Roman origin, situated on the River Seine

•Thirteenth to sixteenth-century cathedral of St Peter and St Paul — beautiful Renaissance façade, fine thirteenth-century stained glass and imposing towers.

•Six churches worthy of seeing, including Gothic St Urbain, Ste Madeleine, and St Jean.

•A Museum of Fine Arts in a former abbey by the cathedral also houses collections of archaeology, natural history and an outstanding library.

•An Historical Museum in the sixteenth-century Hotel de Vauluisant, containing medieval sculpture and the development of the local hosiery industry.

•Picturesque narrow, twisting streets in the Old Town — walk down Rue Emile-Zola, beneath overhanging timber-framed houses.

•Office de Tourisme 16 Boulevard Carnot (Tel: 43 01 03).

ROUTE 1: LAKESIDE AND FOREST CIRCUIT FROM MESNIL-ST PERE

6km; 1$^{1}/_{2}$ hours. A gentle stroll along the waterfront and return on easy forest tracks.

Mesnil-St Père, an ancient settlement, was originally known as Le Grand Mesnil, changing to Mesnil-sous-l'Orient at the time of the Revolution and in recent times being changed again to its present form. Never more than a small village, its indigenous population has grown modestly from sixty in 1620 to close on 400, swelled greatly during the summer by the influx of holidaymakers. Eglise St André boasts a twelfth-century tower, though the remainder of the building is largely seventeenth century.

Today, Mesnil-St Père is one of two amenity centres on Lac de la Forêt d'Orient, the other being Géraudot on the north shore. The village itself is well-provided with restaurants and snack-bars, an hotel, a disco and tourist office, as well as several holiday centres and a nearby campsite.

The Lac de la Forêt d'Orient near Mesnil-St Père

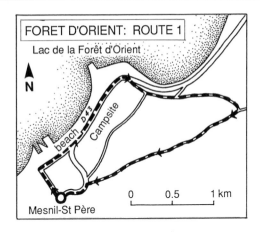

Watersports are the big attraction, particularly sailing and fishing, though there is also a good sandy beach with the customary French beach clubs and holidaymaking facilities. (Since motorised craft are banned, this lakeside situation is refreshingly peaceful.)

From Mesnil-St Père centre, take the road to the right of the church, leading in 300m to the marina. (There is more car parking here and along the waterfront). Turn right along the promenade road, past the tourist office and road junction right. The main beach lies to the left in its shallow bay, beyond which the lake stretches out to the north and west.

At the campsite, look for a conspicuous direction arrow pointing right and follow the track (yellow waymarks) along the campsite and adjacent grounds before entering forest. After 1km leave the track (it rejoins the road in 100m) and turn right on another route, waymarked in orange (known as Circuit Colette).

At the next junction, turn right, picking up the yellow way-marks again. On the left, before approaching Mesnil-St Père now visible ahead, stands a remarkable old oak tree, 59m in height. The D43 road is rejoined at the east end of the village.

ROUTE 2: CIRCUIT OF THE FORET DU TEMPLE

10km; 3 hours. An undulating walk on forest paths and tracks at the heart of the Forêt d'Orient.

NOTE: Not waymarked, but numerous forest rides lead back to the road, never more than 1km distant. The route can be short-cut at several points if required.

This sector of the Forêt d'Orient, to the east of the lake, is thought to have once been under the jurisdiction of the Temple de Troyes, and subsequently that of the Hospitaliers de St Jean de Jérusalem. It is still possible to find vestiges of old dykes constructed by the Templiers; the forestry house which the route passes is known as Maison Forestière du Temple.

A *Route Forestière* (forest road) leaves the D79 about 200m west of the turning to Loge-aux-Chèvres and heads in the direction of Radonvilliers and Brienne-le-Château. Drive along it for about 3km, beyond a track to the left, until the Maison Forestière du Temple in its enclosure is reached on the left.

After inspecting the building, walk back along the road

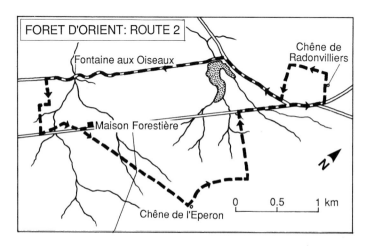

(south-west) for about 100m and take a forest path sharp left (east), rising gently in a straight line. Pass a junction with a path leaving right, cross a stream and a major forest track, continuing ahead with the gradient increasing slightly. The top of the rise is soon reached at a right-angled left turn by a magnificent oak tree — the Chêne de l'Eperon.

Proceed along this left turn for about 750m, past two forest rides on the left, and take a downhill path on the left, crossing a path at right angles and several small feeder streams, to arrive at the road, back along which we started.

A well can be found here as we turn right along the road for 400m. At a meeting of forest roads, continue ahead to a fork. Dienville is signed right, but this route takes the left fork towards Radonvilliers, immediately turning up a forest ride to the left to reach another notable oak tree — Chêne de Radonvilliers.

Shortly beyond it, turn 90° left and take the third forest path left again back to the road. Turning right along it, a marshy lake is approached in about 500m; thereafter follow the forest road for $1^{1}/_{2}$km gently uphill, then down to the Fontaine aux Oiseaux water outlet.

Some 250m beyond, watch for a path left, off the road, leading back to the start of the walk. Before reaching the Maison Forestière, the remains of one of the *digues des Templiers* may be seen on a short path detour.

ROUTE 3: WOODLAND CIRCUIT IN LE GRAND ORIENT, FROM THE MAISON DU PARC FORESTRY CENTRE

10km; 3-4 hours. An ambling walk on forest tracks and minor roads, through delightful woodland.

NOTE: The forest here is a hunting reserve and from 25 October to the end of February walkers are advised to keep to the main tracks and roads: the hunting of animals such as wild boar and deer is a dangerous activity for the casual wanderer to get caught up in. From Easter to 25 October, only the signed restrictions as to access apply — these are mainly to safeguard bird and animal habitats. It is worth noting that the Parc de Gibier peninsula, with its information centre and lookout posts for observing wildlife, is open on weekends and public holiday afternoons and evenings only.

This part of the Forêt d'Orient is renowned both for its wild flowers, mushrooms and fungi and for its lovely stands of oak, hornbeam, lime, beech, aspen, silver birch and hazel.

Inaugurated on 29 October 1973, the Maison du Parc Forestry Centre forms a hub around which activities and life within the nature park take place. It is constructed in style and materials to the design of ancient farm architecture, typically *champenoise* in character.

The barn on the ground floor houses the reception rooms, with information desks and library on the first floor and archival data on the second. What would have been cowsheds contain the permanent exhibitions and projection room.

Photographs, text and exhibits illustrate human interest in the area's resources: extraction of iron ore and greensand, of clay and chalk; the lakes, irrigation and drainage ; forest management , the trees themselves and the flora and fauna whose habitats they sustain.

Situated on the D43 (which encircles the main lake) at the junction with D79, Maison du Parc is a tastefully-

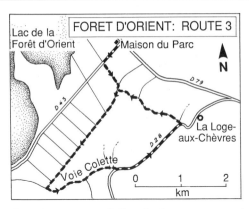

conceived project, open daily all the year round and with helpful staff. A small selection of books, maps and cards is on sale and bicycles may be hired.

From the Maison du Parc (car parking), walk down the D43 towards Mesnil-St Père (south-west), taking the first forest path on the left (waymarked, as elsewhere on this route, in orange). In 500m or so a junction is reached, with direction arrows. Keep right and continue past numerous forest rides to another track crossroads. Mesnil-St Père campsite and the main beach/marina lie about 1½km to the right, but unless they are to be visited, turn first left along voie Colette, the local commune and canton boundary, in the direction of La Loge-aux-Chèvres village.

Skirting the *Bois des Eglands*, keep straight on for some 600m, past a junction right, to arrive at the D28 road between La Villeneuve-au-Chêne and La Loge-aux-Chèvres. A way-mark guides walkers left on to the road, which is followed for 1,500m to a water tower at the west end of La Loge-aux-Chèvres, which may be visited before resuming the walk. (There is a *Gîte d'étape*, a small camp-site and a church here, but no place of refreshment! A short distance to the south lies the Etang du Parc aux Pourceaux, a string of lakes from which the River Barse flows into the Seine.)

At the water tower, turn left off the road and in 300m the forest is re-entered. Our track now leads back to the

Maison du Parc forestry centre

first waymarked path junction on the outward leg. Turn right and when the D43 is reached, turn right again for the Maison du Parc.

ROUTE 4: CIRCUIT FROM AIX-EN-OTHE

14km; 4 hours. An undulating walk on the GR2 waymarked trail and on country lanes.

Reached along the N60 west of Troyes and the D374, the charming village of Aix-en-Othé nestles in the little Nosle valley, one of many cutting into a broad wooded ridge running south-west from Troyes towards Joigny. Tree cover is broken, allowing good views of settlements and countryside. There is a small campsite at Aix-en-Othé, as well as shops selling most supplies.

Leave the village from its east side by the swimming pool, taking the waymarked GR2 path which heads east, connecting villages en route along the Seine valley. The path climbs round north-east and in about 2km enters the

A street in old Troyes

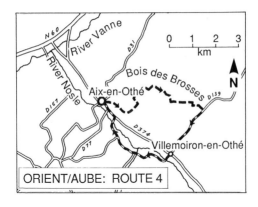

ORIENT/AUBE: ROUTE 4

Bois des Brosses woods.

Ignore a track off right, but when a minor road is reached (D139), leave the GR2 and turn down right, out of the woods. Pass a left junction and reach the hamlet of Villemoiron-en-Othé. The route back to Aix-en-Othé lies alongside the River Nosle on its south bank, past several settlements, finally re-crossing the Nosle near La Vove works to return to the start.

4 Ile-de-France

How to get there

Nearest airports: Paris — Orly or Charles-de-Gaulle.

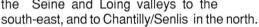

Rail: Fast and frequent connections from channel ports to Paris (Gare-du-Nord). Local services to places along the Seine and Loing valleys to the south-east, and to Chantilly/Senlis in the north.

Road: N7 south-east from Paris to Fontainebleau, or A6 to Nemours. N1/N16 north to Chantilly, or A1 north-east to Senlis.

Area map: I.G.N. Carte Topographique, sheets 21 and 9.

The name Ile-de-France dates back to the tenth century and embodies the idea of the Paris basin, with its huge centres of population and industry, being engirdled by the great plains of Normandy, Champagne, Beauce and Pays de Caux.

Despite the inexorable expansion of urban and suburban Paris out into the surrounding countryside, Ile-de-France is still predominantly a province of farmland and forest. Comprising the departments of Seine-et-Marne, Hauts-de-Seine, Yvelines, Essone, Seine-St-Denis, Val-de-Marne and Val-d'Oise, it is generally considered to have been the cradle of French civilisation and language. Indeed, it is hard to think of a province so richly-endowed with historic towns, châteaux of the French nobility,

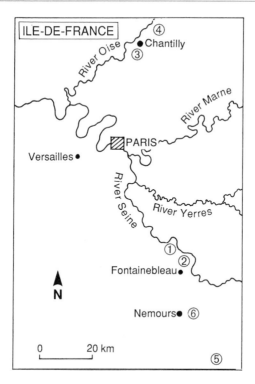

magnificent parks and gardens, great Gothic cathedrals and expanses of hunting forest, the preserve of deer and wild boar (which, however, are protected for sport).

Much of central Ile-de-France is heavily populated, but the peripheral countryside is enduringly attractive to visitors of all kinds, from local day-trippers to holidaymakers on organised or personally arranged trips. Most towns will have a *Syndicat d'Initiative* from which leaflets and maps showing nearby features of interest can be obtained. There are walks of all durations, mostly in easy terrain and only more strenuous where routes cross large areas of forest.

Many visitors come here for the rich sense of antiquity and grandeur which places such as Chantilly and Fontainebleau exude — or for the pleasant rural landscapes and

forest scenery within easy reach of central Paris. Walkers
with the necessary time and inclination can follow sections
of the long-distance footpaths GR1 and GR11 which en-
circle Ile-de-France, linking all the tourist destinations and
historical sites. 'Topoguides' are in French and available
from news-agents and bookshops, but waymarking is un-
equivocal and straightforward to follow with a good map.

Accommodation is plentiful, but in demand during the
high season from mid-July to mid-September when book-
ing ahead is strongly advised. Small hotels abound and
lists are available from local *Syndicats d'Initiative*, or from
the French Government Tourist Office. Campsites in Ile-de-
France are somewhat less numerous than in France's less
populated regions: they are, of course, well-subscribed
during the summer, but walkers with a small tent will rarely
be turned away. There are also numerous opportunities for
riding, golf, tennis, boating and other activities.

The following walks offer a taste of Ile-de-France's diversity. For routes in the south (1,2,5 and 6) a suggested
centre would be Nemours, or one of the small picturesque
towns close to Fontainebleau such as Moret-sur-Loing or
Milly-la-Forêt. For routes in the north (3 and 4), Chantilly or
Senlis are good bases from which to explore the Chantilly
and Compiègne forests

ROUTE 1: CIRCUIT FROM BOIS-LE-ROIS

12.5km; 4$^1/_2$ hours. An undulating walk through forest and past several good viewpoints, with some interesting rock scenery.

Bois-le-Roi, in a region rich in history and legend, comprises a group of villages of Gallo-Roman origin in the Fontainebleau Forest not far from the River Seine. This section of forest has long associations with the kings of France and royal hunts.

The route begins to the south-west of Bois-le-Roi, alongside the D138. It is waymarked throughout in blue and is also path no 12. Take the old embanked Route de Bourgogne, to the right of the Route de la Butte Saint-Louis. Passing through beech trees, climb a gentle gradient and cross over the Ventes-Bouchard track. At the top is a rocky outcrop — Le Petit Rocher — with a small statue of the Virgin Mary in a cleft. A few paces further, on the left, stands a double-trunked oak.

The path descends and turns sharp left, thereafter turning right and mounting to the Butte Saint-Louis (120m) with its chapel ruins. Dropping across the N5 road, climb the pine-wooded slopes of Mont Saint-Germain to reach the little plateau's edge. There are good views over the Seine to the north and signs of trenches from World War I

At the next path junction, turn right, around the flanks of Mont Saint-Germain to an ancient quarry, where the underlying geological structure is particularly clear. Cross the Pavé-de-la-Cave road, after which, contour round the Monts de Truies, with more excellent views north and southeast. A large sandstone monument, one-time gathering point for forest huntsmen and dating back to 1723, is approached at the Grande-Maître crossroads on the Ronde road (130m).

After crossing two valleys, the path circumvents the conspicuous Longues Vallées, past a well-used bivouac cave, to reach the Rocher Canon. It is a fascinating area of rock

In the
Forêt de Fontainebleau

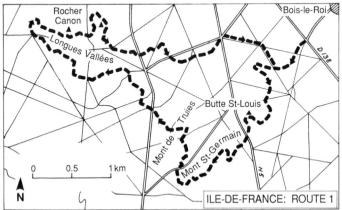

FONTAINEBLEAU FOREST

•The forest stretches south-west from the Seine and is perhaps France's most beautiful area of woodland. Hilly outcrops are of sandstone, while majestic stands of oak and beech, and rocky gorges, are linked by many kilometres of paths which thread through landscapes of sandy desert, moor, cliffs and by swift flowing rivers.

•Take the scenic drive through the area, signed 'Route Ronde'.

•Visit the attractive village of Barbizon, 9.5km north-west and birthplace of the Barbizon school of painting.

•Also see Moret- sur-Loing to the south-east, with its old ramparts and a main street lined with ancient houses. The English painter Sisley lived here for 20 years until his death in 1899 — at 9 Rue du Château. There is an interesting church, and on summer Saturday evenings Son-et-Lumière is put on by the riverside.

forms, including the Tête d'Elephant and Le Menhir. The little massif's summit is bouldery and bare and leads the walker past a huge block equipped with steps for views down the stony slopes below.

Descending south from Rocher Canon, the path gradually turns eastwards, crosses the Ronde road again and passes holly trees to the Chailly-Samois road. Beyond, the N5 is encountered. To return to the start, take a path immediately right of the Chailly-Samois road, over the Ventes-Bouchard track crossroads and back across the Butte Saint-Louis rise.

ROUTE 2: TOUR OF THE ROCHER CASSEPOT

6km; 2 hours. A circuit of a mostly wooded rocky eminence, not far from the banks of the River Seine.

To the south-west of Samois-sur-Seine, there is road access to Tour Denecourt and ample car-parking.

A sign (path 14) indicates the start of the path from
the esplanade in front of Tour Denecourt. The route drops
west across a slope and continues over rocks and in pine
trees. At the base of a small hill, keep ahead and cross
the metalled Jean-Bart road, then over a junction, continuing amongst dwarf oaks and silver birch to the D116.
Follow the north crest of Rocher Cassepot in bushy veg-
etation, crossing three successive tracks until, after a final
rocky stretch, the fourth track is taken down left and over
the Rocher-Cassepot road. Climb in forest towards the
line of rocks ahead. At the top, there are yellow waymarks
and a sign for walk 15, which touches 14 at this point.

Keeping left, the red and white waymarks of the long-

The Palais de Fontainebleau — Cour Henri IV

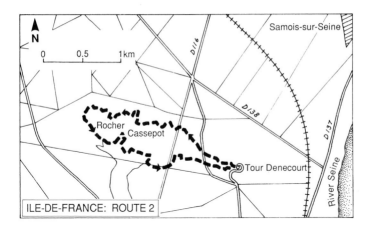

ILE-DE-FRANCE: ROUTE 2

distance GR1 Ile-de-France walk are encountered and followed east on a good forestry track along to the summit
edge amid pines. Soon, an excellent viewpoint is reached,
left, at the Grand Point du Rocher Cassepot (110m).

Descending south, path 14 soon reaches the Constan-
tin crossroads and takes a route left, parallel to the Vallée
de la Solle road. The D116 and a rocky passage are passed
and the Jean-Bart road crossed, before the path finally
returns over rugged ground to Tour Denecourt.

North of Paris, on the edge of a game-stocked State
Forest Reserve, stands elegant Chantilly, renowned for its
lace, china and *crème Chantilly* (whipped cream), and more
especially for its magnificent château. Begun in 1560 and
later enlarged, the complex includes stables, a library (with
fifteenth-century illuminated manuscripts) and the great
Musée Condé, containing a rich collection of paintings, tapestries, stained glass and precious stones.

The formal lake and gardens which surround the buildings are the work of the famous landscape gardener, Le
Nôtre: Chantilly was a forerunner to his *pièce de résistance*
at Versailles.

Nearby will be found one of France's most beautiful race-
courses and a very fine golf course. The whole area is
popular with holidaymakers and has earned the reputation

WHAT TO SEE AT FONTAINEBLEAU
(9km to the south-east)

•Dating from the sixteenth and seventeenth centuries, this is one of France's most historic châteaux. French rulers from Louis VII to Napoleon III lived here and developed the palace buildings.

•Cour Ovale is an outstanding French Renaissance arcaded courtyard. On its south side is Salle de Bal, built by François I and magnificently decorated; included is the 54m-long Galerie de François.

•A double 'horseshoe' staircase dating from 1634 leads to the first floor and Napoleon I's apartments, with Empire furnishings. Other magnificent rooms include the Queen's and King's Apartments, the latter with ceiling paintings and tapestries.

•Within the beautiful gardens are found the 'Carp Lake', 'Jardin Anglais' and a Parterre with ponds and statues by the famous French landscape artist Le Nôtre. The park contains a maze (*labyrinthe*) and vine-covered trellises, while Henry IV's Grand Canal stretches a full kilometre through the landscape.

of being a fashionable destination for visitors.

Not far to the east of Chantilly lies the ancient town of Senlis, with an exceptional length of Roman wall — 840m long and bearing sixteen towers. Most of the French kings resided at Senlis' great royal castle: today there is a Hunting Museum in the grounds, adding to its attraction.

The adjacent Cathédrale Notre-Dame, started in 1153, embodies all phases of Gothic architecture from the twelfth to the sixteenth centuries, and is well worth seeing. The remainder of Senlis is made up of fascinating narrow streets and alleyways.

Both towns are connected on the GR11 Grand Sentier de l'Ile-de-France. However, an interesting approach which

Galerie Henri II in the Palais de Fontainebleau

explores more of the surrounding forest can be made from Orry-la-Ville to the south, and there is more fine walking to the north around the Forêt d'Halatte to the ancient city of Pont-Sainte-Maxence.

ROUTE 3: ORRY-LA-VILLE TO CHANTILLY OR SENLIS

12km; 3 hours to Chantilly. 13km; $3^1/_4$ hours to Senlis. A gently undulating forest route past lakes, to either of two historic towns of great interest and charm. (This walk can easily be reversed if required.)

Orry-la-Ville/Coye is on the Paris (Nord) to Compiègne railway line. Turn left (north-west) outside the station and pick up GR1 waymarks (this is a long-distance circular footpath round Paris called Sentier de l'Ile-de-France.) GR12, which we follow, is concurrent with GR1 for a while.

After a 500m stretch alongside the railway, turn right on the first track and walk through forest as far as the Grandes Ventes crossroads. Here turn left and watch carefully for a path half-right from the St Ladre junction some 500m ahead. This leads down to the first of the Etangs (lakes) de Comelle. The four lakes are fed by the River Thève — fish-

Château de Chantilly

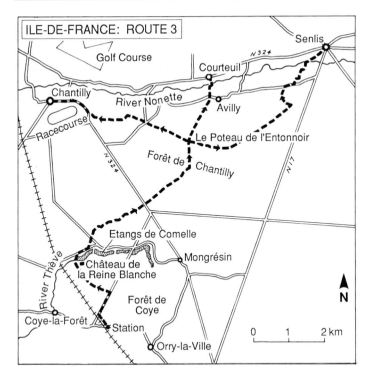

ing is possible but bathing is prohibited. Rising above the
first lake (La Loge) is Château de la Reine Blanche (Castle
of the White Queen), a hunting lodge built in 1828 by the
Duke of Bourbon.

At the start of the dam, GR1 heads off along the south
bank and our route now continues north from the lodge,
over the dam and along a metalled road to the right. At the
second junction, turn left and immediately right, on to an
ancient Roman way from Senlis to Soissons, known as
Chausée Brunehaut.

We are now in the Forêt de Chantilly, today owned by
the Institut de France, having previously belonged to
powerful families — the Bouteilliers, the Montmorencys
and the Condés. Henri d'Orléans, Duke of Aumale and
fourth son of Louis-Philippe, finally donated the forest to

PLACES OF INTEREST IN CHANTILLY AND SENLIS

Chantilly

•To the west of the town stands an exceptionally elegant château, reflected in a formal lake.

•The eighteenth-century Grand Stables and nearby racecourse are prestigious and very popular. (NOTE: The château is open every day except Tuesdays, and race days, but only weekends in winter).

•The whole complex is owned by the Institut de France and houses the famous Condé Museum, with priceless paintings, stained glass, tapestries, manuscripts and precious stones, notably the Condé Rose Diamond.

•Park and gardens, laid out by Le Nôtre, were a forerunner of his more extensive work at Versailles. The rustic hamlet contains a 'winter garden'.

•5km south in a forest clearing are the Commelles Lakes. Just, north of Chantilly a golf course surrounded by beautiful woodland.

•St Leu-d'Esserent, on the right bank of the River Oise is an attractive village close to stone quarries from which Versailles and Chartres Cathedral were built. The village has a remarkable twelfth-century abbey church.

Senlis

•An ancient town with a royal history dating from AD987.

•The eighteenth-century former priory in the grounds of the old castle houses a Hunting Museum.

•The twelfth to sixteenth-century Notre-Dame Cathedral is notable for its 80m spire, a fine Gothic carved doorway, Romanesque west façade and a lofty interior with gallery.

•Gallo-Roman remains can be seen around the castle perimeter and in the Arena, outside the ramparts. The best-preserved Roman wall in France — 840m long, with eighteen surviving towers.

•There are many narrow streets and alleyways and lovely old houses down towards the River Nonette.

the French State. It covers about 2,100 hectares and is planted predominantly with oak, beech and lime, home to 200 stags and does.

Continue along the Roman way which veers north-east and cross the N324 road. Kilometre markers now line the route and the quiet, observant walker may spot deer in this section. 1,500m further on, take a path left and arrive at Le Poteau de l'Entonnoir crossroads.

Here a decision must be taken to visit either Chantilly or Senlis. For the former, turn left and follow GR11 waymarks through forest and out to parkland on Chantilly's eastern flank, thereafter passing close to the famous race-course and reaching the east end of the town (4km).

For Senlis, turn right, again following GR11 waymarks, as the route skirts the Avilly racecourse and associated enclosures, turning north then north-east to the town centre (5km).

A shorter alternative conclusion to this walk would be to continue on GR12 from Le Poteau de l'Entonnoir on a lovely forest path, emerging to cross a road just west of Avilly racecourse, and to enter Courteuil via an old stone bridge over the River Nonette.

Hunting Lodge,
Château de Chantilly

ROUTE 4: CIRCUIT TO PONT-SAINTE-MAXENCE FROM AUMONT-EN-HALATTE

28km; 7-8 hours. A longer walk with more frequent ups and downs on good forest tracks, visiting an ancient city. Aumont has an interesting fifteenth-century church, a Musée Henri Barbusse, as well as a café, restaurant and some shops.

Turn left in front of Aumont's church on the GR12 route and, beyond the cemetery, go right, climbing a sandy track to a crossroads (spot height 128m). Here turn right to reach the Arthus crossroads, thereafter following a winding path on a steep wooded hillside below Monte Alta (142m), leading to the Route d'Auteuil, one of five major forest arteries.

Turn left and walk down this forest road to the Déroute junction and, 200m beyond, go left along a well-marked path through beech and hornbeam. This is a variant of GR12 providing access to Pont-Sainte-Maxence.The following section round Fleurines is rather complex and needs to be navigated with care.

Cross the D565 in a northerly direction then cross the Route des Bouleaux, shortly afterwards turning right along Route des Suisses. Cross the Batis road and in 1km turn left down to thePetite Carrefour junction, continuing north over it and crossing the Route de la Mare aux Oiseaux.

Further on, after about 500m, turn right down the Route du Diable, descending the hillside in a big 'S'. Once over the road to Beaurepaire, a steep slope is climbed into the Petite Cavée woods. Take the first track on the right and in 300m turn left, going right again before a descent is made to the Oise valley. A metalled road is reached, followed for 200m, and a narrow path taken off left, dropping to Pont-Sainte-Maxence.

This ancient city is named after an old bridge over the Oise, and after an Irish virgin martyred here. There is a fifteenth-century church, the Abbaye de Montcel, foun-

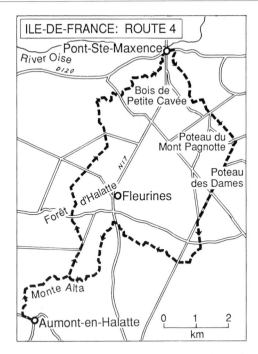

ded in the fourteenth century by Philippe le Bel, and the Calipet mill, standing on its panoramic viewpoint. The town is well-provided with hotels, eating places and shops.

Continuing the circuit, leave by the street opposite the railway station, cross Place du Maréchal de Lattre diagonally and walk down Rue de la République. The Oise is crossed; turn left. In 300m go right, down Chemin de Calipet, rising into the Chapelle-Saint-Jean woods. Turn left down Route de la Montignette and in 400m turn right on a small road to the Hétéroclite signpost. A lovely forest path continues to the Mont Pagnotte junction, the highest point in this forest at 216m.

Proceed south-west for 600m, back on the main GR12 routing, and at the Poteau des Dames intersection, carry on ahead, crossing the D120 road and in 1km reaching Croix de St Rieul. A path goes south over a tarred road, becoming less distinct for a while as it veers right and joins a track to the Poteau des Blancs Sablons. Contour along north-west for 1,500m and turn left to the *Chêne à l'image* viewpoint. Here the route drops straightforwardly to the north-west, out of forest, and crosses the N17 main road.

Fleurines lies 500m off route to the right, at the heart of the Forêt d'Halatte. Traditionally a hunting centre, there are fifteenth and sixteenth-century churches, hotels/restaurants and some shops.

Passing the Maison Forestière de Fleurines, we enter forest and undergrowth again, walking to the south round a forestry house and up on to the crest of Monte Alta. The Route d'Auteuil, met on the outward leg, now takes us directly back to Aumont-en- Halatte.

Typical forest scenery of the region

ROUTE 5: A CIRCULAR WALK FROM FERRIERES

13km; $3^1/_2$-4 hours. An undulating walk up a shallow valley, through a varied landscape past old mills and farms.

Ferrières' ancient origins date back to a flourishing Benedictine abbey, its name to a once-thriving iron and steel industry. Today, it is a charming town, dominated by the remarkable St Pierre-St Paul church and the Notre-Dame-de-Bethléem chapel opposite.

On the right bank of the River Loing, this walk unfolds across fields and woods in a shallow valley, utilising in part the GR13 long-distance footpath which runs from Ile-de-France to Bourgogne. Follow GR13 waymarks on the outward leg, yellow discs on the return.

Leave Ferrières from Place des Eglises and climb left of the abbey church to pass through the tower archway. Emerging at the Convent Yard with its ancient covered well and pottery workshop, pass through a porch into the old town. Go right (towards Montargis) along a plane-lined avenue, at the end of which rises the elegant fifteenth-century cross of Ste Appoline. Turn right into Boulevard de la Brèche and cross the River Cléry on an old stone drain.

Arriving at the Trois-Platones crossroads, turn left into the D115, leaving it in the middle of a hill to follow the GR13, sharp left after the poplar trees on a track to Court Epée farm (muddy after rain).

The track nears the river, fringed by 100-year-old willows, and soon Corbelin hamlet appears to the right. Go left, following the river for 400m before reaching a metalled lane. Turn left and come to an unusual Gothic bridge (the Gril de Corbelin).

Follow the lane to a left bend then take a narrow, grassy track right, turning left before a hedge to meet the D815 road from Pancourt to Griselles. There are cafés and a few shops at the nearby village of Griselles.

Crossing a road, keep ahead on a tarred lane past a

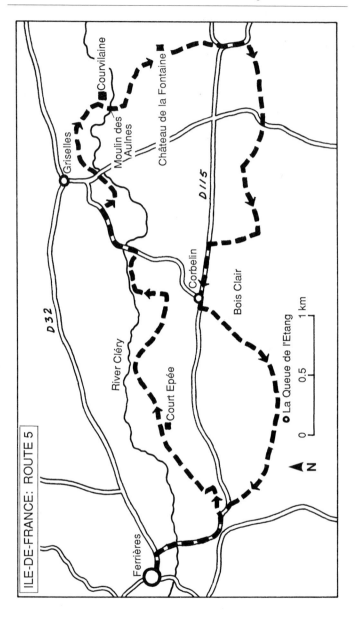

ILE-DE-FRANCE: ROUTE 5

```
┌─────────────────────────────────────────────────────────┐
│  WHAT TO SEE IN                                           │
│  MONTARGIS                                                │
│  30km to the south                                       │
│                                                           │
│  •A town of many bridges, over    •Twelfth and fifteenth-century │
│  its river, canal and lake.       château walls and ramparts.   │
│                                                           │
│  •A good sixteenth-century        •A local history museum in    │
│  church choir.                    the Town Hall.               │
└─────────────────────────────────────────────────────────┘
```

ruined mill, veering right to approach Courvilaine farm, characteristic of the architecture in this part of France. Turn right at a wall corner (signed 'Moulin des Aulnes') and pass another ancient mill before crossing a canal by footbridge. Follow the wall on a narrow dyke, then cross the River Cléry itself on a footbridge, followed by a marshy stretch.

Further on, a clear stream is encountered — a spring rises on the left by a wash-house. GR13 now meets GR132 which leaves here towards Courtenay and Villeneuve-sur-Yonne. Continue on GR13 up a stony track alongside the Château de la Fontaine grounds (the building is modern). Beyond a large farm on the right, Bois-le-Roi hamlet is reached.

A classical-style château stands on the corner of the D115 and, further on, there is a small chapel on the left. Leave the road where the GR13 proceeds ahead over fields, but turn right, following yellow discs along a pleasant track through undergrowth. Cross the D815 road in a hollow and climb to a cultivated plateau on the other side, keeping along the edge of woods.

At a copse, turn right to the D115 road and turn left into Corbelin hamlet. At its far end, go left towards the trees of Bois Clair (private — keep to the track!), emerging at a lane near La Queue-de-l'Etang. Following a small valley, the walk reaches the D115 again and it is but a short stroll back to Ferrières.

ROUTE 6: CIRCUIT OF THE ROCHER DE BEAUREGARD

2km; 1 hour. A walk over several rocky outcrops above the River Loing, with good views over Nemours and surrounding countryside.

The group of rocky summits lies to the south of Nemours in a park of unexpected rock formations and debris. Nemours itself, 15km south of Fontainebleau, is a pleasant little country town, with an elegant sixteenth-century church, ancient houses and a twelfth-century castle which houses a museum.

Leave Nemours centre along the N7 towards Souppes and shortly after the château on the banks of the Loing, turn left along Rue de Beauregard, past a housing development. Opposite this, turn left on Chemin du Crot-aux-Loups and next right on Chemin de Crèvecoeur. A track leaves this left just by the Pain de Sucre and zigzags up to a small plateau edge at spot height 125.8m. There is a good view from here over the town, Mont Delo to the north and the surrounding rocky landscape.

The GR13 long-distance path is now followed southwest, leaving behind the rocky terrain for heathland and veering south away from the plateau edge. Dropping through trees, we cross the Nemours to Poligny road, leaving GR13 which continues left, and instead carrying straight ahead, following yellow waymarks. A modest path leads through a rocky depression and undergrowth, passes an interesting rock fault and climbs to the old *table d'orientation* on Rocher de Beauregard, erected years ago by the Touring Club de France and now rather badly worn. Despite summer tree foliage, views are lovely, while in winter they are extensive, especially over the River Loing with its poplars and fishing shacks.

Descending to the right of a large boulder, a plaque can be found commemorating a Frenchman called Doigneau who, from 1867 on, painstakingly uncovered many pre-

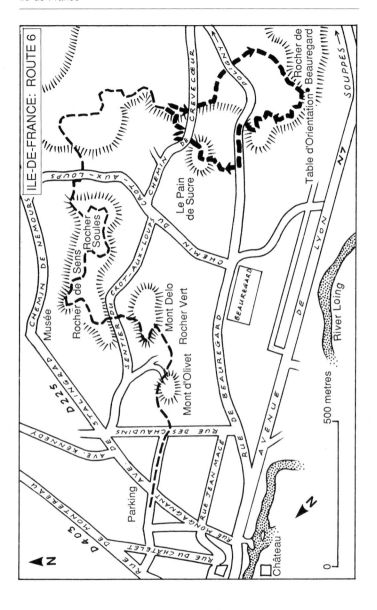

ILE-DE-FRANCE: ROUTE 6

FEATURES OF
INTEREST IN NEMOURS

•Sixteenth-century church
and old houses.

•A Museum in the twelfth-
century castle, with its four
towers and square keep.

•Fine river views from the
town's main bridge.

•Cycles can be hired from
the station, to explore the
country north and into
Fontainebleau Forest.

Church at Nemours

historic objects, now on show in Nemours Museum. Continue along the plateau edge to a clump of broom and bear right, regaining the edge and dropping gently. Opposite a tall pine tree on the right is a man-sized rock which moves when touched or blown by a strong wind — La Roche Tremblante.

A descent now begins from Le Gros Mont on to more rocky ground and the Nemours-Poligny road is followed left for 100m. Take a narrow path right, in an acacia wood, and attack the short climb to Le Pain de Sucre's pointed summit. A few stones here indicate the site of a former cottage — L'Ermitage. The way down includes a covered pathway, ending in a few steps, and soon the starting point on Chemin de Crèvecoeur is reached.

(**NOTE**: The GR13 runs from Nemours town centre over the main outcrops and would make an interesting linear walk of about 4km, steep and scrambly in a few places. Alternatively, footpaths like the one described above can be taken to any of the tops and linked together at will.)

5 Pays de Caux

How to get there

Nearest airports: Le Havre

Rail: Services from Rouen to Yvetot and Le Havre, and south from Dieppe, the nearest channel port.

Road: A13 'Autoroute de Normandie' from Paris and over the

Pont de Tancarville. N27 south, and D925 west from Dieppe, and the D940 coast road from Le Havre. N28 and N29 south-west from Abbeville.

Area map: I.G.N. Carte Topographique, sheet 7.

Pays de Caux is a vast chalk plateau occupying much of Seine-Maritime department in the northern sector of Normandy. It is largely devoted to agriculture and is often reminiscent of parts of southern England — a landscape of big, rolling fields, low wooded ridges, farmsteads and villages. The texture and colour of fields throughout the year are a visual delight, as are the wooded valleys and the architectural details within settlements.

Architecture in this part of Normandy is notable for its high-sweeping slate roofs and great bluntly-wedged gable-ends. Clay being a common raw material, it is not surprising to find brickwork is made into a feature, often built into chequered and herringbone patterns between exposed timbers — hallmarks of the Norman façade.

Several pretty rivers flow west to the sea, their valleys

green fingers in an open countryside. The plateau which
they drain is ancient limestone from the ocean bed, hun-
dreds of metres thick, laid down by inundations of the sea
about 6000BC. The subsequent layers of wind-blown soil
covering the chalk is rich in organic debris and provides the
foundations for successful dairy and arable farming.

At the coast, the Caux plateau ends abruptly in steep
limestone cliffs of exceptional beauty — the so-called Côte
d'Albarte (Alabaster Coast). Beneath these soaring white
walls and their ancient hanging valleys (*valleuses*), run
pebbly beaches and a string of small resorts, all very popular in summer. The most stunningly attractive of these is
Etretat, cradled between sensational cliffs with arches and
a needle rock 70m high.

Dieppe and Fécamp appeal for contrasting reasons,
being bustling maritime towns with busy harbours and historic buildings. At Dieppe in particular there are excellent
shopping streets and a Saturday market. Etretat, Dieppe
or any of the intervening smaller resorts would make good
centres for exploring Pays de Caux on foot; so also would
villages inland up the Durdent or Saâne valleys.

Pays de Caux has several long-distance footpaths running across it. The coastal route (GR21) divides well into
day-walk sections linking resorts, thus enabling walkers to
return to the start by bus or to be picked up by car. Most
places contain small hotels and a campsite, so any number
of stages can be joined together into continuous walks
with overnight accommodation halts en route. The total
length of the GR21 coast path from Etretat to Berneval is
100km.

Associated footpaths penetrate the Caux plateau itself,
weaving complex but waymarked routes on paths, tracks
and lanes through the distinctive detail of a fascinating
agricultural and pastoral landscape. Notable north-to-south
routes are the GR211 from the Seine to the coast at
Veulettes-sur-Mer; and the GR212 along the Saâne valley
from Ste Marguerite.

Weather in Pays de Caux is often fresh and invigorating,
with heaviest rainfall in the autumn and sunshine hours

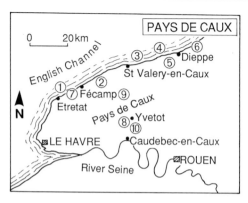

generous throughout the spring and summer. Because the walks often use farm tracks and cross fields and woods, the going underfoot can be muddy. Stout walking shoes or boots (but perhaps not wellington boots, except on the shortest of routes) are advised, as are a windproof jacket (especially in cool weather or early and late in the season), a spare sweater, waterproofs and a little energy food in reserve.

Few of the routes stray far from human habitation, though not all hamlets and villages possess a shop. Resorts on the coast can all be relied upon for buying provisions or obtaining meals and drinks, in the main summer season from June to September anyway. Buses connect the principal places on the coast, as well as some inland locations, but services should be verified before setting out with the intention of using them.

Finally, timings for the walks allow for occasional stops for a snack or photograph, and for slower progress on hills. Because the routes are often complicated, directions appear in considerable detail, often at the expense of description. Though waymarked with the familiar red and white paint flashes of the French long-distance paths, careful note needs to be taken of turnings and natural features in some areas, to avoid losing the path.

ROUTE 1: ETRETAT TO FECAMP

13km; 3^1/$_2$-4 hours. A fine clifftop walk on good paths, linking two resorts of major interest on the Côte d'Albarte. Level walking much of the time but several descents to sea level involved. Waymarked with red and white flashes and GR21.

Etretat, of all the Côte d'Albarte resorts, is richly endowed with natural beauty and its popularity is fully justified. The little town, running back between the Aval (up-stream) and Amont (downstream) cliffs, is self-contained and caters well for visitors. There is a reconstructed, though authentic, covered market hall, and the Notre-Dame church is worth a visit. Etretat was once the haunt of painters and writers who came here to enjoy the special clarity of light and unsurpassed coastal scenery. For the limestone cliffs which rear up to north and south are, indeed, remarkable: soaring walls, pinnacles and arches and inaccessible little bays beneath dizzy drops.

Before leaving Etretat on the coastal route, climb to Falaise d'Amont from the promenade's eastern end and visit the Nungesser-Coli museum, dedicated to the memory of two French aviators who died while attempting to fly across the Atlantic in 1927. Nearby stands the Notre-Dame-de-la-Garde chapel with its conspicuous slender spire.

The route begins from behind the Roches Blanches hotel and climbs to the clifftops, proceeding clearly ahead with small undulations to the village of Bénouville, where there are cafés and one or two shops. Beyond the church, turn left, branching left again to reach the Valleuse du Curé. Keep to the clifftops as far as La Haie d'Etigue's beach access, whereupon turn right towards the car park and immediately left.

Passing enclosures as it climbs again to the plateau edge, the route skirts Vattetot-sur-Mer and turns left on to the D211 down towards Vaucottes beach. Angling up the

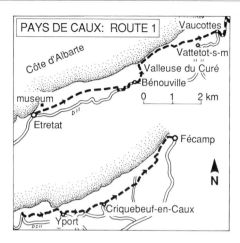

other side, the road doubles back sharply right and we take a path off left, quickly leading to Yport. This modest holiday centre has an unusually large beach at low tide, with rock pools and a small harbour.

Take the street opposite the jetty and, beyond the

Etretat's Porte d'Aval arch and Needle Rock

WHAT TO SEE IN
NEARBY LE HAVRE

•The port was founded in the sixteenth-century by François I to replace a silting-up Harfleur. During World War II it became Europe's worst bomb-damaged port but was rebuilt to the designs of Auguste Perret, contemporary of Le Corbusier and a pioneer of reinforced concrete construction.

•City-centre modernism includes living units over shops and offices, broad, open boulevards and squares, and Perret's own St Joseph's church.

•The André Malraux Museum of Fine Arts on the seafront contains works by Renoir, Corot, Dufy, Picasso, Sisley, Léger, Boudin and others.

•Museum of old Le Havre in a seventeenth-century house in the St François quarter near the Bassin du Commerce.

•For sportsfields, a boating lake, ice-rink, golf course and campsite, visit the Forêt de Montgeon, 700 acres of woodand to the north of the city.

•Twenty-seven kilometres of docks are arranged around a complex of basins, and boat trips are available to view quaysides and shipping activity.

•Office de Tourisme: Place de l'Hôtel-de-Ville (Tel: 21 22 88).

village square, turn left on a narrow track winding upwards again on to the plateau. At a Calvary by the D211 road, keep left and continue past Criquebeuf-en-Caux. Waymarking is less clear for some 700m but reappears on the drop to Grainval. Climb out the little valley by a restaurant and keep ahead (north-east) through a campsite ground to enter Fécamp from alongside its beach.

Fécamp is France's principal cod-fishing port, its economy dependent upon associated industries such as canning, ship repairing, fertiliser production and net and rope manufacture: it does not make many concessions to tourism! Nevertheless, the harbour is often busy with fishing and leisure craft, and scuba divers use the surrounding clear waters for their sport.

Fécamp is noted as the birthplace of Guy de Maupassant and as the home of Bénédictine liqueur — the distillery and museum are found in Rue Alexandre-le-Grand. The abbey church of Ste Trinité is well worth visiting; it is one of France's largest churches and contains a relic in the Sanctuary of the Precious Blood which attracts large numbers of pilgrims.

Le Havre's modernistic city centre

ROUTE 2: FECAMP TO PETITES DALLES

16km; 5 hours. A walk through three Pays de Caux coastal villages. Four descents are made to sea level valleys, with subsequent ascents to the plateau. Can be muddy in places after rain. Waymarked with red and white flashes, GR21.

Leave Fécamp on the Sente des Matelos, situated to the west of the northern harbour quay. From the Notre-Dame-du-Salut seamen's chapel and beacon, an excellent view-point, take the cliff path as far as Val de la Mer and follow this valley up right to Senneville and the D79 road. (Alternatively, walk along the D79 itself from Fécamp.)

There is no cliff path between Val de la Mer and Val Ausson, the terrain being dangerous and therefore cordoned off. From the crossroads at the east end of Senneville, branch left and watch for a track sharp left descending Val Ausson towards the sea. Near the bottom, a path climbs up to the clifftops and reaches the village of Eletot, with a café and a few shops.

Keeping parallel to the coast, our route reaches a farm

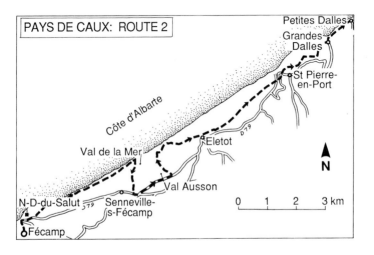

PAYS DE CAUX: ROUTE 2

Petites Dalles
Grandes Dalles
St Pierre-en-Port
Côte d'Albarte
Eletot
D79
Val de la Mer
N
Val Ausson
N-D-du-Salut   Senneville-s-Fécamp
Fécamp
0   1   2   3 km

Fécamp

and continues ahead towards the distant church tower of St
Pierre-en-Port. Above the beach access point at St Pierre,
turn left towards the cliffs, skirting the village to pass some
villas before following the path ahead and reaching a track
coming from the D79 road. Turn left for 25m, then right,
and continue to the edge of the Hêtre valley. Here turn off
left, then right, to descend into Les Grandes Dalles.
Tucked down in its wooded combe, this tiny resort and
Les Petites Dalles are especially picturesque. To reach the
latter and the conclusion of this route, leave Les Grandes
Dalles opposite the fountain and follow a fence north,
climbing to the cliff edge and dropping to Les Petites
Dalles.

ROUTE 3: ST VALERY-EN-CAUX TO ST AUBIN-SUR-MER

15km; 4-5 hours. An interesting and varied route above the Côte d'Albarte cliffs, linking several resorts.

NOTE: If the coast path is not passable for safety or access reasons, detours are waymarked in yellow. Otherwise waymarks are red and white flashes and GR21.

St Valery-en-Caux, with its own Falaises d'Aval and d'Amont, echoes Etretat. Both cliffs are crowned with war memorials and it was here in 1940 that the 51st Highland Division made its epic last stand. Many Highlanders are buried in the Commonwealth War Graves cemetery just outside the town.

Leave St Valery from its east end via the old customs track, which is followed for 2km along the plateau by the cliff edge. At this point, a possible short inland detour (yellow waymarks) turns right along a boundary to the N25 road, which is taken for 1.5km before turning left and left again

Cliffs and beach at St Valery-en-Caux

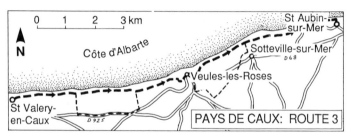

PAYS DE CAUX: ROUTE 3

back to the coast path and a waymarked track down to Veules-les-Roses.

The limestone cliffs are stained delicate shades of brown each side of Veules-les-Roses, a sleepy, sun-faded sea-front which comes to life in the summer with families and children. An alternative to the cliff path now follows the river a little way inland and at a major road junction takes the Rouen road (N25) for 50m before going left up between houses. Once on the plateau, turn right and in about 500m, left on to a stony track which crosses the D68 and leads down into Sotteville-sur-Mer, a village of Viking origins. There are eating places and shops here.

Go towards the sea and turn right on the coast path, a rough track parallel to the cliff edge, for 1.5km. Continue ahead on the surfaced lane at Epineville, crossing the shallow Saussemare valley and arriving in St Aubin-sur-Mer, a summer resort with hotels, restaurants, shops and beach.

WHAT TO SEE IN
ST VALERY-EN-CAUX

• Originally a trading and fishing port, the town was severely damaged in 1940.

• A monument to the British Army stands on Falaise d'Amont to the right of the harbour; a monument to the 2nd French Cavalry stands opposite on Falaise d'Aval.

• This popular resort has a safe beach and is also a yachting centre.

• The restored Renaissance house on the quayside was once visited by Henry IV.

• Commonwealth War Cemetery just outside the town.

ROUTE 4: QUIBERVILLE-PLAGE TO POURVILLE-SUR-MER

12km; 3^1/$_2$-4 hours. A largely wooded walk with numerous gradients but on good paths and tracks, leading past access to some notable buildings and natural features. Waymarked with red and white flashes, GR21.

Quiberville-Plage leads along a bright seafront with seafood stalls and high-prowed, colourful fishing boats to the charming village of Ste Marguerite. Traditionally the holiday retreat of many painters, today it is a picturesque resort with a flower park and a fine unspoilt Romanesque church.

Follow the beach east and pass the path off right along the Saâne valley (the GR212 — see Route 5). Shortly after this junction, take a path right past trees to Ste Marguerite itself. In the village, turn left and immediately right on a surfaced track through woods and turn left towards Phare (lighthouse) d'Ailly. Now keep right on the D75 road, descending past villas at Vasterival and entering a wooded valley. After some bends at the valley bottom, take a path ahead up through more woods and on to the D27, which is followed left to a very interesting church. At the lane end, it is mostly a fourteenth-century structure but there are many twelfth-century Romanesque features inside, and the 'Tree of Jesse' stained glass window by the artist Georges Braque; he died in 1963 and his tomb lies in the cemetery.

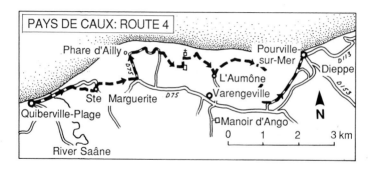

(A short distance south along the lane is the Parc Floralies des Moutiers — remarkable landscaped gardens containing many rare plants and trees and open to the public.)

Just before the cemetery, our route turns right on a track
still among trees, dropping to a *valleuse*, one of many
ancient hanging valleys left by a retreating coastline. At
Rue de l'Aumône hamlet, take a track left which becomes
a path dropping towards a steep declivity. This is crossed
and the Bois des Saules left for Le Hamelet settlement.

A short way west stands the Manoir d'Ango, a well-
restored late-Gothic complex built in 1530 by Jehan Ango,
shipbuilder and Governor of Dieppe. It is a fascinating
structure, almost orientally extravagant and containing a
great domed dovecote. Allow about half an hour each way
to visit it.

Passing north of Le Hamelet's château, a good lane
leads down to the beach at Pourville-sur-Mer. Two kilometres beyond, continuing on the coast path towards

The Côte d'Albarte (Alabaster Coast) at Pourville-sur-Mer

Dieppe, a museum of World War II military vehicles stands on the cliff tops in mute testimony to Dieppe's role in 'Operation Jubilee', the first Allied reconnaissance landing in Europe. Many Canadian commandos and supporting troops died on the fateful day — 19 August 1942 — but valuable lessons were learned for the main Normandy landings two years later. Canadian monuments and flags in Dieppe and its surroundings mark the tragic loss of life.

Typical Pays de Caux landscape

ROUTE 5: STE MARGUERITE TO BRACHY, OR ANGLESQUEVILLE-SUR-SAANE

12km; $3^1/_2$ hours (if extended, 26km; 8 hours). A pleasant walk with gentle gradients along a river valley, passing many settlements. Woodland provides good shade, but paths are muddy after wet weather.

The route, waymarked GR212, starts at the east end of Quiberville-Plage and follows the true right bank of the River Saâne. At Le Fond de Longueil, a loop left, then back right, brings us to the church. 100m beyond, a track is taken left, past Le Vieux Château, veering east then south, first to cross the main D925 road, finally meeting it at the entrance to Ouville-la-Rivière (hotel/restaurant).

At the village crossroads, walk along the D152 for about 2km and at the end of Ribeuf woods, fork left then right to pass a chapel. A path now leads to Gueures village, at the south end of which take the path ahead alongside a wood, then crossing fields to meet the D108 into Brachy. This concludes the shorter version of the route. For those with more time, the walk can be extended with no difficulty by continuing on the GR212.

Keeping to the east slopes of the Saâne valley, follow the waymarked path through St Ouen woods, keeping to the metalled lane for 1km and passing by Rainfreville on the other side of the river. At a dairy, turn left on the D107 and in 200m go right on the D507 for about 100m. Fork right now on to a wooded path and at the D147, continue ahead along the wood edge.

The route now stays between trees and river all the way past Auzouville-sur-Saâne (hotel), Thiédeville and Imbleville to reach the walk's end at Anglesqueville-sur-Saâne (hotel/restaurant, shops, swimming pool).

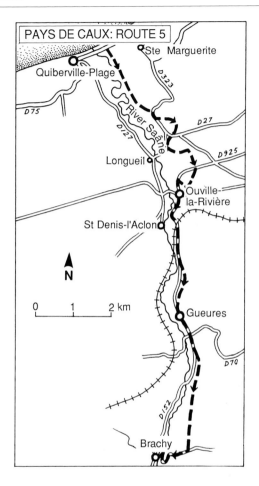

PAYS DE CAUX: ROUTE 5

ROUTE 6: DIEPPE TO BERNEVAL

10km; 3$^1/_2$ hours. From a superb cliff-top viewpoint over
Dieppe, a rural walk crossing two valleys at the edge of the
Caux plateau.

Dieppe is France's oldest seaside resort and well worth
exploring in its own right Its prosperity founded on
shipping and maritime adventure, the town-centre docks
still form its *raison d'être.* Here too are old streets and
buildings, including the impressive Château with its interior
museum containing Impressionist paintings and an exceptional collection of carved ivories from the 1600s. The
Grande Rue shopping area is transformed into a huge open
air market every Saturday — the best of its kind in northern
France.

   To the east of Dieppe's harbour, follow the streets of Le
Petit-Fort and La Bastille up to the cliff tops. The route
passes the fishermen's Chapelle Notre-Dame-de-Bonsecours, a magnificent viewpoint over Dieppe's harbour
complex and the River Arques estuary.

Dieppe —
Port de Voyageurs

PAYS DE CAUX: ROUTE 6

Taking Rue-A-Blanc, meet the D113 road and follow it east for about 1km, before turning left on to a stony track descending to the diminutive beach at Puys. Climbing left from the Canadian War Memorial, a road is taken to a pedestrian crossing. Cross to the left and reach the Roman Camp de César, thereafter following the path along to Bracquemont, a small rural settlement with a café.

To avoid an often muddy track, turn right opposite the cemetery and circumvent the village to the south. In the square, turn right, then immediately left on to the D100 and take the first track left. This crosses a road at Le Bout-du-Haut, an extension of Bracquemont, and continues north, crossing and recrossing the D113 several times to reach Belleville-sur-Mer.

An earth track leads to the Val du Prêtre and the sea's edge, after which our route climbs on to the cliff tops and in a right-angled turn drops to Berneval, the official northern terminal of the GR21 long-distance coastal footpath, and the end of this walk.

WHAT TO SEE IN AND AROUND DIEPPE

Dieppe
•The Grande Rue shopping street, with clock-towered Café des Tribunaux and Puits-Salé well; Saturday market.

•The imposing Château contains Impressionist paintings, model ships and carved ivories from the seventeenth century when Dieppe was a centre for this craft.

•City-centre docks — for cross-channel ferries, fishing and commerce — are lined with arcaded shops, bars and fish restaurants.

•A pebbly beach is backed by pleasant lawns, gardens and sporting facilities.

•There is an excellent panoramic viewpoint at the chapel of Notre-Dame-de-Bonsecours, on cliffs to the east.

•Dieppe contains many lively shops, cafés, restaurants; there is a casino, a good selection of hotels and nightlife.

Pourville-sur-Mer (3km west)
•World War II museum, with military vehicles & weapons.

Varengeville-sur-Mer (8km west)
•Parc Floralies des Moutiers — gardens with many flowering shrubs, rare plants and trees and a house built in 1898 by Sir Edward Lutyens.

•The twelfth- to fourteenth-century church on the cliffs contains a stained glass window by the cubist painter Georges Braque, who is buried outside.

•Just to the south stands Manoir d'Ango, a beautiful, restored late-Gothic building built by Jehan Ango, shipbuilder and governor of Dieppe, in 1530. There are steep roofs, elaborate façades and a large, domed dovecote.

Arques-la-Bataille (6km south-east)
•An imposing eleventh-century castle on a rocky hill above the town — one of Normandy's most important feudal remains. Its unspoilt keep and ramparts are encircled by a path, all above the Béthune valley.

•There are walks in the nearby Forêt d'Arques, trout-fishing at Martin-Eglise and water sports at Varenne to the south.

ROUTE 7: VILLAINVILLE TO YPORT

17km; 5 hours. A varied walk, complex but waymarked, on paths, tracks and country lanes. The route passes farm-steads and villages and enters woods, before descending from the plateau to the small seaside resort of Yport. (Way-marked GR21b, red and white flashes.)

From Villainville village (café, shops), the walk leaves the D39 road and follows a track east, crossing the D74 at Le Moulin and proceeding ahead to Cuverville (café, shop).
   Turn left by the Epicerie and go down towards a farm,

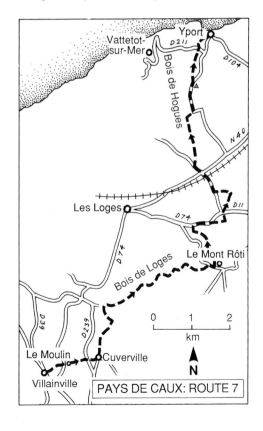

PAYS DE CAUX: ROUTE 7

turning left on to a lane opposite a wood. Where the lane bends left, enter the woods ahead (Bois des Loges) along their lower edge. Our path now contours along throughout the woods' length, emerging beyond a hunting lodge, whereafter it skirts right, along the edge of open land to reach the D79 road and Le Mt Rôti village.

Just past the bus stop, turn left before a farm and at the top of the hill, turn left, then right. The lane bends left and passes an electricity sub-station; continue straight on between two farms. Where the path ends at another farm, go left to a junction between the D11 and D74. Here, a narrow, stony track is taken on the right, becoming grassy and meeting a surfaced lane. Turn left to meet the D11, along which turn right, over the railway and the D940 (buses for Etretat and Fécamp).

Continue on the D11 for about 250m, forking right on to a grassy track near another electricity sub-station and descending into a wood (Bois des Hogues). Veer right, climbing to a lane, along which go left. Nearby is the naturist Club Gymnique de la Porte Océane.

From the trigonometric point 97m, the walk eschews the road down through woods to Yport, choosing instead a grassy path left. At the top of Yport, take the first street right, then Rue de la Gardine and Rue de Jean Feuilloley to the village centre.

ROUTE 8: CAUDEBEC-EN-CAUX TO ALLOUVILLE-BELLEFOSSE

14km; 4$^1/_2$ hours. From a delightful riverside town, an undulating walk through forest and over fields on good tracks,
to an old Pays de Caux settlement.

Caudebec-en-Caux, situated on a particularly scenic curve
in the Seine, near the huge Pont de Brotonne suspension
bridge, is historically the capital of Pays de Caux. After
severe fire damage in 1940, it was rebuilt in the form of a
great amphitheatre, but one corner of the old town es-
caped and provides a fascinating glimpse of the
past, as far back as the thirteenth century.

There is a fine fifteenth-century church with an
internationally known pipe-organ, and a large museum
dedicated to the writer Victor Hugo. His daughter Leo-
poldine and her husband were drowned in 1843 by the
tidal bore known as *le mascaret*, though engineering work
on the Seine's banks since then has reduced the bore's
size and capacity for damage. Caudebec has a broad riverside promenade, lined with gardens and hotels, and is a
pleasant spot from which to view the busy river traffic.

Leave Caudebec at the Calidu on the GR2 west of the
town, and cross the N182 road. Proceed west through
trees for about 500m and turn right twice, on a forest track
veering round north along the Ste Gertrude valley. In 3km,
turn right and cross a small bridge to enter Ste Gertrude.

Take the D40 west for 150m, then turn right on a path to
meet a woodland track, right, which is followed for 2km
through forest (Forêt de Maulevrier). Near L'Ouraille hamlet, take a path west up and over into a small valley, climbing out to the forest edge. The route now drops through
forest again and turns right along a valley bottom for about
800m, thereafter climbing to La Houssaye and a track
along the forest edge. This leads to crossroads at Le
Boscabosc, where we turn left, then right (north-west) on
a way across fields and meadows. At a surfaced lane, turn

PLACES OF INTEREST ALONG THE LOWER SEINE

Lillebonne
•Second-century amphi-theatre — one of France's most important Roman ruins, still used for open air performances.

•Gallo-Roman museum opposite in the Town Hall.

Pont de Tancarville
•One of Europe's great suspension bridges (1959).

Villequier
•A small, historic riverside town; Victor Hugo's daughter and husband are buried in the medieval church, which also contains superb sixteenth-century stained glass.

•There is a large museum dedicated to Victor Hugo.

Caudebec-en-Caux
•The town's riverside prom-enade is lined by hotels and gardens, ideal for watching river traffic.

•In the fine fifteenth-century Notre-Dame church is a 2,300-pipe organ, built in the reign of François I; also sixteenth-century stained glass windows and statues.

•The rare thirteenth-century Maison des Templiers houses a museum of local history.

Pont de Brotonne
•Second of the Seine's big suspension bridges (1977).

Parc Régional de Brotonne
• A small, forested wilder-ness of 17,000 acres on the south bank, midway between of Le Havre and Rouen. A protected zone of beech, oak and pine, with few roads, so good for walking and riding.

•There is a craft centre north-west of Bourneville and a Museum of Ecology at Le Trait to the north-east.

St Wandrille Abbey
•Founded in AD649, the now magnificent ruins are set in shady grounds.

•The present monastic church, in the form of a tithe barn, was moved here piece by piece from Neuville-du-Bosc, 50km away, in 1969. Gregorian Chant is still used at Mass and afternoon Vespers.

Jumièges Abbey and promontory
•A site of outstanding beauty — the abbey ruins have two octagonal towers rising 43m.

•There is a museum in the Abbot's Lodge, and a small pottery.

•Jumièges promontory is especially beautiful during apple-blossom time called the 'floréal' (mid-April to mid-May).

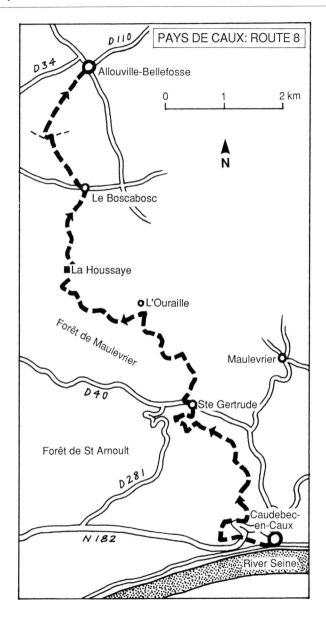

PAYS DE CAUX: ROUTE 8

D 110

D 34

Allouville-Bellefosse

0   1   2 km

N

Le Boscabosc

La Houssaye

L'Ouraille

Forêt de Maulevrier

Maulevrier

D 40

Ste Gertrude

Forêt de St Arnoult

D 281

Caudebec-
en-Caux

N 182

River Seine

left and immediately right to reach Allouville-Bellefosse.

The Allouville-Bellefosse oak, with chapels built into its massive trunk system, is 800 years old and a tourist attraction of some note. The village also contains a sixteenth-century church, as well as a hotel and restaurant.

Duclair's ferry across the Seine

ROUTE 9: HERICOURT-EN-CAUX TO CANY-BARVILLE, OR VEULETTES-SUR-MER

18.5km; 5-6 hours. Crossing and recrossing the verdant valley of the River Durdent, a walk through well-settled countryside, with good views over this part of Pays de Caux. An optional extension to the coast.

Waymarking (GR211) starts at the sportsground and the walk takes the D233 left, then the first track on the right. Cross the D149 to St Riquier and climb on a sunken path curving west. At a track junction, turn right, cross the D233 and continue along a stony track, turning left on to a lane bordered by beautiful beech trees alongside the River Durdent.

Skirting woods, cross the D106, proceeding ahead to join the D105, crossing the bridge right, and climbing towards the church in Auffay. At a road junction up on the plateau, turn left in front of the Château and continue for some1$^1/_2$km before dropping left through woods to Le Hanouard. Cross the Durdent and take a track right, then climb left, thereafter going north-west towards the lower edge of a wood.The route leads on, in 2km, to Grainville-la-Teinturière (hotel/restaurant).

Pass north through the village and climb left in woodland. Beyond La Roquette settlement, take the second turning left, a narrow track descending to Barville, with its tiny church so delightfully situated. Keep on down to cross the river, with good open views of the Château de Cany and its surroundings (not open to the public).

At the railway level crossing, go right along the D131 in trees, taking a track left up to La Ruelle hamlet and thence right along and down to Cany-Barville (hotel, restaurant, campsite).

If desired, the route can be extended to a long day's hike by continuing on the GR211 to the coast at Veulettes-sur-Mer (add 10km; 3 hours).

From the village's west end, take a path up through

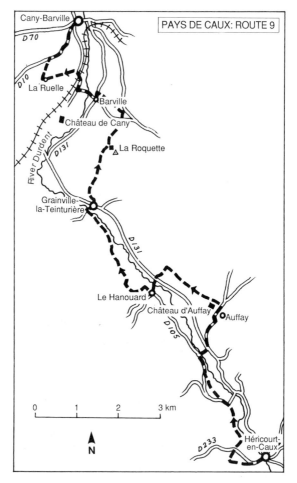

PAYS DE CAUX: ROUTE 9

woods and across to Clasville. Follow the D271 right, and at the crossroads, the D69. Short-cut a hairpin bend on the descent to the Durdent valley by turning off left. This crosses market-garden terrain and meets the D268 near Paluel. Cross the D68 ahead and continue on a track along the valley's west side to Veulettes-sur-Mer, at the mouth of the River Durdent — a pleasant resort with shops, restaurants and hotels.

ROUTE 10: CAUDEBEC-EN-CAUX TO YVETOT

14km; 3$\frac{1}{2}$-4 hours. A walk connecting an attractive riverside location on the Seine with a Pays de Caux market town, passing en route some typical Pays de Caux buildings and scenery. Waymarked GR211a.

The walk starts at Maison Forestière de la Haie des Prés, about 1km north-east of Caudebec-en-Caux (see Route 8 for description). Take the second grassy track right, beneath power lines, passing close to trigonometric point 116m. At La Haie des Prés, go right on a lane, then left past some beautiful dovecotes. At the crossroads, keep right on a track which crosses the main road towards the Pont de Brotonne suspension bridge and continues by descending into woods.

*Château de Clères
and its wildlife park*

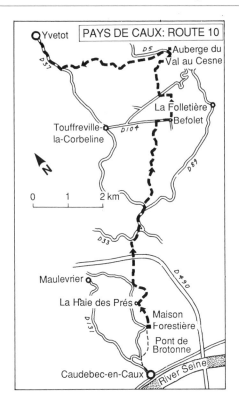

Cross over the D33 and walk along the D89, left, to a junction, keeping left towards Touffreville for about 200m before turning right on to a track along a wooded valley, past a very picturesque manor house on the right, finally meeting the D104. Go right, then left at Befolet hamlet, left again after 400m, then right down into woods (undergrowth can be dense).

Turn left along the D5 and watch for a grassy track off left (just beyond the Auberge du Val au Cesne), almost parallel to the road. Fork left after 2km, following another valley to a water purification station, whereupon the D37 leads in 1km to the outskirts of Yvetot.

This sizeable town was completely rebuilt after being badly damaged in World War II and is now a major agricultural

---

NEARBY PLACES OF INTEREST

Clères (36km east)

•A long-established zoo and a wildlife park at the château, with free-roaming birds and animals.

•The village has half-timbered fifteenth and sixteenth-century houses, castle ruins and an old, covered market.

•There is a vast Musée des Automobiles de Normandie, containing everything from an 1878 steam driven fire-engine to aircraft, from pre-1900 bicycles to racing cars and military vehicles; also a collection of motor cars from 1895 to the present day.

---

market centre for Pays de Caux. It is also known for a huge stained glass window by Max Ingrand in its St Pierre church.

6 Suisse Normande and Forêt des Andaines

How to get there

Nearest airports: Le Havre and Rennes

Rail: Local services south from Caen to Flers, Domfront and La Ferté-Macé/Bagnoles.

Road: D562 south from Caen to Thury-Harcourt and Clécy. N158 south from Caen to Falaise then D909/D19 to La Ferté-Macé and D916 to Bagnoles-de-l'Orne.

Area Map: I.G.N. Carte Topographique, sheet 18.

Not far south of Caen in the Calvados department of Normandy, the River Orne cuts through ancient rocks of the Armorican Massif which underpin the land from here west to Brittany. Between Thury-Harcourt and Putanges-Pont-Ecrepin, the Orne meanders through gorges, wooded valleys and steep-sided hills. River bends have carved steep cliffs, while here and there an isolated higher summit rises more conspicuously.

The French call this region *Suisse Normande*, though any resemblance to Switzerland borders on fiction! Indeed, this is pretty, hilly countryside rather than impressive and mountainous; it is a good place for walkers, canoeists, anglers and even rock-climbers.

Thury-Harcourt is an excellent base for excursions along the River Orne, and is sometimes referred to as the 'Gate-

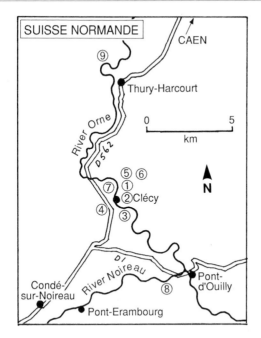

way to Suisse Normande'. However, Clécy is more of a
central hub, and there are a number of interesting short
walks to local beauty spots in the vicinity. The surrounding
countryside is highly picturesque, with many walking possibilities, while Clécy's sixteenth-century Manoir de Placy
houses antiques and a local Crafts Museum; a miniature railway and associated museum in the park will appeal specially
to youngsters.

35km to the south, over the border in Orne department,
lies the spa town of Bagnoles-de-l'Orne and the Forêt des
Andaines. Bagnoles and neighbouring La Ferté-Macé are
exceptionally pleasant towns and form the suggested
centre for this chapter.

Bagnoles-de-l'Orne, largest spa in western France, re-
ceived royal patronage as long ago as the sixth century and
during the Edwardian era was immensely fashionable. The
town's inevitable decline since those halcyon days has
been partially reversed by its growing reputation as a reju-

venating and curative spa: sulphuric and radioactive waters are claimed to help cure glandular and circulatory ailments.

The town is a bustling, cosmopolitan place, with many restaurants, salons de thé and high class shops. The spa itself, on the left bank of the River Vée, is often crowded with well-heeled Europeans eager to bathe in the water from the Great Spring which gushes out at 27°C and has a flow rate of 11,000 gallons per hour.

A gleaming white casino and luxury hotel are reflected in Bagnoles' town-centre lake, whose banks are laid out to gardens and fringed with willows. Sporting provision in the area is generous, including tennis, swimming, boating, shooting, fishing and golf. Walks in the Forêt des Andaines are dealt with after those in Suisse Normande.

Both Clécy and Bagnoles-de-l'Orne become very busy with visitors during the summer season, though it is always possible to walk away from any crowds, either into the hills or into the forest. Spring and autumn are favoured seasons to come here — accommodation is in less demand, the landscape is colourful and the quality of light particularly beautiful.

Clécy

Suisse Normande

ROUTE 1: SEBIRE HAMLET FROM CLÉCY

4.5km; 1½ hours. Country lanes with views over typical Suisse Normande countryside.

Leave Clécy via Rue Notre-Dame, cross the N562 and walk along the road leading towards Château de Pontécoulant (signed). After about 400m, take the Basse Bigne lane on the left and pass through the village. At the top of the little hill is a panoramic view over surrounding countryside.

Descend to the right, past a few houses and a stream and, arriving at a road, turn right to Sébire hamlet. Turn right again for a more direct return to Clécy.

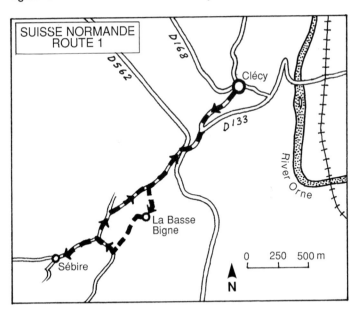

ROUTE 2: CIRCUIT TO
LA CROIX DE LA FAVERIE

3km; 1 hour. A short walk ending by the River Orne.

Leave Clécy by Rue de la Poste, turn right at the restaurant and car park, and at the top of the slope go right again. After a few metres, turn left and at the top of a small hill on this road take the track as far as a little meadow. Another left turn and 300m of walking leads to a picnic area.

From here, continue to a small wood with a magnificent view over a viaduct and the River Orne. Still keeping left, drop down a steep path to the river bank. To return to Clécy, use a fairly steep track on the left, facing the weir, coming out opposite the park. Higher up to the right is the road leading back to Clécy via the Post Office.

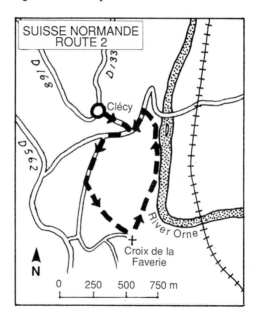

ROUTE 3: LA LANDE CLECY

7km; 3 hours. Easy country lanes connecting little hamlets
and starting alongside the River Orne.

At the bus stop in Rue de la Poste, turn left: there are views
of the rocky eminences known as La Butte au Physicien
('Doctor's Hill') and Le Pain de Sucre ('Sugar Loaf'). To the
left is the Leisure Park and in the river bend the Manoir
de Placy (see introduction).
Now follow the Orne to the viaduct (small boats for hire),
after which continue on the road as far as the second level
crossing. Turn right immediately after, pass behind the old
station building and at the end of this road, go right.
Return to Clécy is through Bertheaumes village, proceeding to Les Cages hamlet and thence down into Clécy, seen
delightfully from above.

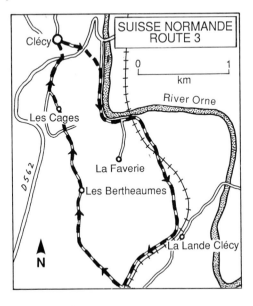

View from Roche D'Oëtre

ROUTE 4: L'EMINENCE FROM CLECY

7.5km; 3¹/₂ hours. A climb to one of Suisse Normande's excellent viewpoints. Mostly along lanes and tracks.

Turn left at the last houses on the road towards La Landelle, as far as the N562. Turn right at the top of the hill and watch for a signpost indicating 'L'Eminence 282m' on the left. From the summit, views, in good visibility are very far reaching, extending to Caen.

For the return leg, retrace steps to the farm and turn right, descending for 1km to Sébire hamlet. Go left again, along a lane to a Calvary, cross over the N road and enter Clécy near the cemetery.

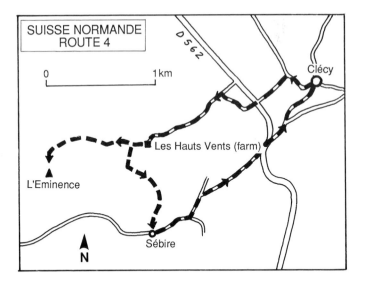

ROUTE 5: CIRCUIT FROM CLECY TO EGLISE ST REMY AND LA LANDELLE

7km; 3 hours. An easy walk along country lanes close to the River Orne.

Leave from the *Syndicat d'Initiative* (Tourist Information), turn right and descend towards the Orne, crossing through the village of Cantepie. There are some fine willows on a riverside property, and hang gliders use the slopes above in suitable weather conditions.

Go left over the railway and follow the road to La Croix, turning right up a shady incline; the climb is rewarded by beautiful views from the top.

Drop down to St Rémy church, which is twelfth century and well worth looking at. The walk continues left, round the perimeter of the cemetery and down to the N562 road. At the level crossing, keep left, taking the N road for 500m

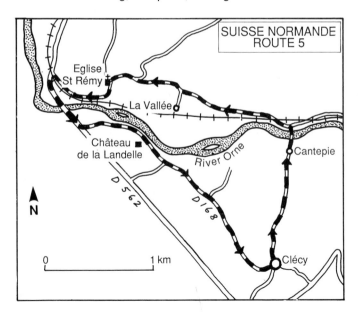

— this can be a trifle hazardous in heavy traffic, particularly on the bend.

Cross the Orne on Pont de la Landelle and take the first road left — a shady, winding walk past a lovely property on the right. Clécy is reached with recently cleared views over the lower part of the village.

Pain de Sucre, near Clécy

ROUTE 6: PAIN DE SUCRE FROM CLECY

5km; 2 hours. A walk using the GR36 path, leading to a superb viewpoint.

Leave Clécy in the direction of Pont-du-Vey, crossing the Orne and continuing ahead towards Le Vey church. (Pont du Vey's old mill, with its great splashing waterwheels, is now an inn.)

Take a track before the church and then the first path on the left, leading up to the summit of Pain de Sucre. Because of its situation, there are exceptional views over Clécy and the Orne valley from this top.

Leave by a steep path towards the river and the village of La Serverie. Cross the railway line, turn left, then right to cross the Orne on Pont de Cantepie. This road heads back to the centre of Clécy

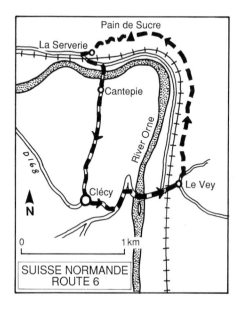

Pain de Sucre
La Serverie
Cantepie
River Orne
D 168
Clécy
Le Vey
N
0   1 km

SUISSE NORMANDE
ROUTE 6

ROUTE 7: CHEMIN DU HAUT DES ROCHERS DES PARCS

5.5km; 2 hours. A path along rock outcrops above the River Orne.

Start from Clécy towards Pont-du-Vey, cross the Orne and take the first road right, leading to the campsite. Opposite the entrance, take a track left which leads up to Le Haut des Rochers.There are excellent vistas over the Orne valley.

Continue as far as a small car park, turning left and proceeding ahead until a secondary road is met, whereupon turn left towards Le Vey. Re-cross the Orne for the clear way back to Clécy.

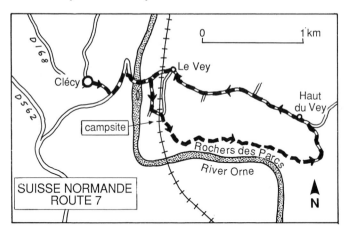

PLACES OF INTEREST AROUND SUISSE NORMANDE

St Rémy
•Remains of old iron-ore mining installations. Good views from cemetery of hilltop church.

Clécy
•Though a small town,dubbed 'Capital of Suisse Normande' — a centre for touring and for walkers, rock-climbers and anglers. There are numerous local walks to beauty spots, including the Pain de Sucre (Sugar Loaf), L'Eminence viewpoint and Croix-de-la-Faverie. A 10km 'Route des Crêtes' links many of these features along minor roads.

•1km east is Pont-du-Vey, with its old mill (now an inn) and splashing waterwheels.

Mont Pinçon (south of Aunay-sur-Odon)
•A 365m-high vantage point over the 'bocage' to the west.

Château Pontécoulant (near Condé-sur-Noireau)
•Seventeenth-century, state-run building set in a landscaped park with fishing lake. Its interior is now a museum with much fine furniture.

River Noireau
•From Pont-d'Ouilly, a small touring centre and important crossroads, the river runs beneath high escarpments west to Pont-Erambourg where it joins the River Vère.

Roche d'Oëtre and St Aubert Gorges
•South of Pont-d'Ouilly is an interesting area of rocky gorges cut by the River Orne. Dominating is Roche d'Oëtre, a sensational lip of vegetated cliff 120m above the Orne's densely wooded valley. Reached from the D301, there is a car park and refreshments.

ROUTE 8: PONT-D' OUILLY TO PONT-ERAMBOURG

13.5km; 3¹/₂-4 hours. An undulating walk over small hills, past attractive hamlets and along wooded river banks.

A pleasant village situated at the confluence of the rivers Orne and Noireau, Pont-d'Ouilly takes its name from the old, seven-arched bridge which, from the twelfth century on, carried the main road from Mont-St-Michel on the border with Brittany to Rouen, via Lisieux and Falaise. This traffic fostered a thriving population of innkeepers and carters, explaining the presence of a chapel on the site of the present-day church, erected in 1925.

Administratively, the village was divided by the rivers into two hamlets, dependent respectively upon the communities of St Marc d'Ouilly and Ouilly-le-Basset: their amalgamation to form Pont-d'Ouilly followed bombing and damage in 1944. Today, visitors will find a few hotels/restaurants, some shops and a campsite nearby.

From the village, cross the River Orne and walk along the D511. Just beyond the church, two long-distance paths leave in different directions: GR36 (Manche to Pyrénées) goes south towards Menil-Hubert and GR221, which we

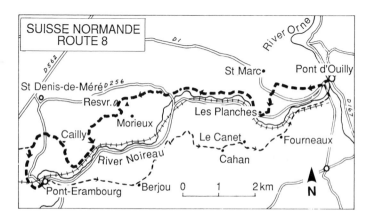

*William the Conqueror's
birthplace, Falaise*

follow, goes west on a tarred road. (The northern leg of GR36 branches off right towards Thury-Harcourt.)

Our road soon becomes an earth track and climbs to the first of several hilltops. About 500m before the village of St Marc, turn left (south), over the D1 road and drop towards the River Noireau. Arriving at the D511 road, go right (west), through Les Planches hamlet (hotel) and, before the road bridge, turn down right on a stony path between houses and river.

Continue along a pleasant track beneath steep woods, a road is reached and followed alongside the Noireau as far as La Martelée hamlet. Cross the river and railway line and in 100m take a stony track on the left, climbing a hill (spotheight 202m). Before the small reservoir, turn left (south) on to a road descending to the Morieux-Bénusse lane (there is a *Gîte d'étape* at Morieux, run by the Camping Club of France).

The GR221 now takes the road right (west) and beyond Bénusse hamlet turns left and descends on a track to the valley. Go right, alongside the railway and climb once again to pass through the hamlet of Cailly. The lane leading northwest soon cuts across the D56 and in 400m, just short of Le Vaux hamlet, reaches a junction with GR226 — one of its termini, the other being the bay of Mont-St-Michel.

FEATURES OF INTEREST AT FALAISE AND CAEN

Falaise (18km east of Pont-d'Ouilly)

•The birthplace of William the Conqueror. His castle is one of Normandy's earliest and most imposing, with a keep, massive round towers and flanking walls above the River Ante valley. The interior and dungeons are open to the public.

•Good shopping streets and market, and large statue of William the Conqueror in the town's cobbled main square.

Caen (26km north of Thury-Harcourt)

•Historic city, linked to the sea by the Caen Canal.

•Duke William's castle here has rampart views, two fine museums (Fine Arts with paintings, engravings and decorative arts; and Normandy Folklore with farm-life, costume and local handicrafts).

•Abbaye-aux-Dames — the tomb of Mathilde, Duke William's wife; multi-columned crypt.

•Abbaye-aux-Hommes — Duke William's tomb and much of architectural interest.

•Old houses and pedestrian-ised shopping precincts; numerous markets. Excellent sports facilities.

•Dockside walks for views of shipping and the River Orne.

•Office de Tourisme: Place St Pierre (Tel: 86 27 65).

To reach Pont-Erambourg, keep left (south) back to the River Noireau.

A recommended extension to this walk is to follow the blue waymarks of the GR221 variant from Pont-Erambourg, back to Pont-d'Ouilly, via Berjou, Cambercourt, Cahan, Le Canet and Fourneaux — an extra 10km, about 3 hours. Thus the complete circuit would make a good day's walk of some 23km.

ROUTE 9: CIRCUIT FROM THURY-HARCOURT

26km; 6-7 hours. An undulating walk through typical
Suisse Normande countryside, over hills, through woods
and hamlets.

From Thury-Harcourt's town centre (shops, hotels, restaurants, campsite), cross the railway and the River Orne,
and at the junction with the D166 turn right for 200m,
watching for a sharp fork left (south-west), waymarked
GR36. The track climbs to a hilltop, with excellent retrospective views across to Thury-Harcourt, continuing over
the crest and past woods to St Benin hamlet.

Ignoring all junctions off, keep ahead (west), gently uphill
on a lane, and at a bend, leave it for a path right which
contours round before dropping then veering left (south-
east) and climbing over a wooded ridge to meet a road and
enter St Martin-de-Sallen (café, supplies).

Leave south-west of the village centre, still following
GR36 signs along a newly-made track. 500m on, at the
edge of the Bois de Culey, GR36 forks sharp left (south-
east). Our walk now follows the GR221A west, along the
edge of the wood then into it, staying on the ridge top for

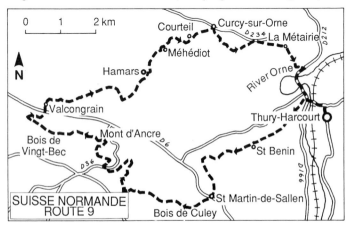

WHAT TO SEE AT THURY-HARCOURT

•'Gateway to Suisse Normande' and much rebuilt since war damage in 1944. Its thirteenth-century church retains its original façade, but the eighteenth-century château of the Dukes of Harcourt was burned to the ground and the ruins are now surrounded by pleasant public gardens.

•Signposted circuit of Suisse Normande countryside for motorists and cyclists links Thury-Harcourt with St Martin-de-Sallen, Culey-le-Patry, St Lambert, St Pierre-la-Vieille, Clécy, St Rémy, St Omer and Esson. Scenery is of rocky bluffs, isolated hill-tops, patterns of hedges and fields on both sides of the River Orne.

---

about 2km.

Beyond a replanting zone, descend right (north) and in 500m turn left (west), cross a stream and reach the D36; walk along it right for 100m before turning off left across a felled area. Soon, the route turns right (north) along a small valley and at the forest edge goes west again, over a small stream, thereafter continuing on the steep northern slopes of wooded Mont d'Ancre.

When the track descends through Bois de Vingt-Bec, look out for a sharp right turn on to our return leg variant, waymarked with blue rectangles. Drop down across the D6 and at Valcongrain hamlet, turn right (east). Walk along delightful wooded hillside, pass the ruins of La Cour mill and climb a small valley north-east to Hamars village (inn/-restaurant, food shop). The hamlet of Méhédiot is followed by Courteil, both at a valley head, and a lane is joined leading to Curcy-sur-Orne.

Proceed south-east over a hill to a lane near Le Val Gosse, turning left along it and taking a path right off the next junction, this leads in about 1km to La Métairie.

Thury-Harcourt lies some 3km to the south-east and the GR36 is soon encountered and followed, dropping steeply to the River Orne, which is crossed twice on a big bend. Lanes bring the circuit towards its conclusion as the Orne is crossed for a third time and Thury-Harcourt is approached.

Forêt des Andaines

This mixed forest is of major amenity value to this part of the
Orne department and its leisure use is actively encouraged.
During the French Revolution, the Andeyne and La Ferté-
Macé forests were amalgamated; even so, changes in land
use and ownership have reduced its area to 5,437 hec-
tares, from a total of 8,038 hectares in 1674.

Resistance activities during World War II, associated with
the 'Falaise Pocket' to the north, seriously damaged the
tree stock, the worst-affected areas being replanted with
beech and conifers. Traces of the fierce fighting and bombing from 1942-4 still exist in certain parts of the forest.

The Forêt des Andaines,19km long and from 2 to10km
wide, occupies a roughly NW-SE position, echoing other
Normandy forests on similar hills, such as Perseigne,
Ecouves, Pail, Multonne, Monnaye, La Motte, Mortain and
St Sever. Average altitude in the Andaines forest is 200m
above sea level, rising to 308m on the Route Forestière du
Mont-en-Gérome, near Le Rond des Dames.

Streams flow between undulating hills, and several
valleys hold stretches of water, some natural, some man-
made. Occasionally, streams run in deep gorges, such as
those of La Cour, Villiers and La Vée, and all waterways
flow to the Mayenne River, thence into the Loire. Rivers
and ponds contain trout, pike, carp, perch and eels,
though fishing is usually by permit only and is forbidden
altogether in some waters.

Amongst birds to be seen or heard are the cuckoo,
pigeon, turtle dove, jay, crow and many other woodland
species, including falcon on the forest edge and ducks and
small waders near water.

Stags live here and are hunted each year; roe deer are
less common while wild boar populations fluctuate from
year to year. Many other mammals typical of mixed woodland habitats are to be found: hares, weasels, polecats,
stone martens, foxes and badgers.

Like many areas containing wildlife, the Forêt des

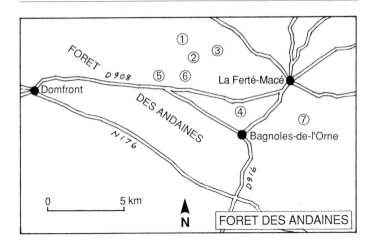

Andaines is vulnerable to abuse by carelessness: fire is a real threat and creatures can be easily disturbed by noisy or thoughtless behaviour.

The forest is criss-crossed by some 38km of public roads and 32km of forestry roads, 16km of stony tracks and 69km of forest rides and earth roads or paths. There are a number of walking trails, mostly waymarked and averaging 2 to 3 hours duration; horseriding itineraries are also being established.

ROUTE 1: CIRCUIT OF
LA CHAPELLE-DES-FRICHES

3km; 1 hour 15 minutes.

From the big crossroads hub — Carrefour de l'Etoile — take the Route de la Sauvagère road and after 3km watch for a signpost on the left at the edge of forest to La Chapelle-des-Friches. Three hundred metres along this track is car parking.

Walk along the track following the forest edge to the left, past a small meadow on the right. A short distance ahead stands the chapel, built a century ago close to the village which was then an important fortification. The chapel was a focal point of many pilgrimages and the seats outside the entrance allowed a swelling congregation to follow the services taking place. Inside are a few statues, notably that of St Ortaire who was summoned throughout the area to cure pain.

To return to the car park, continue ahead for about 300m and take a track left, leading to the Sommière de la Noë de Livet and back to the start.

Bagnoles-de l'Orne

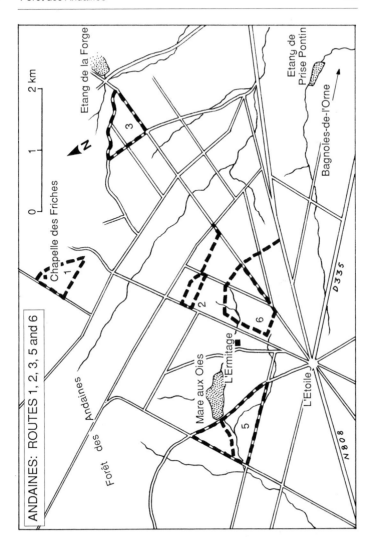

ANDAINES: ROUTES 1, 2, 3, 5 and 6

ROUTE 2: CIRCUIT DE L'ERMITAGE

$3^1/_2$km; 1 hour 30 minutes. (See map page 155.)

From the crossroads south of L'Ermitage lake in the forest centre, walk along the Sommière Sud de l'Ermitage to the St Paul crossroads, turning right along the Coulonche forestry road and crossing the Vivier stream valley. Take La Messe track, right, to L'Ermitage itself, site of a once cultivated clearing and farm occupied by monks from Lonlay-l'Abbaye for several centuries.

Turn right at the lake's west end, passing magnificent stands of varied tree species — this leads back to the start.

VARIANT: (Circuit of La Messe)From the Carrefour des Châtaigniers (chestnuts): walk south-east then turn sharp left along Chemin de la Messe. This old track was used by

forestry workers in the past, on their way to church at Champsecret. At L'Ermitage lake, turn left back to the start. There are good forest views and this small circuit could be added on to the main walk — allow an extra hour.

Forêt des Andaines

ROUTE 3: CIRCUIT OF LA MARE AUX OIES

4km; 2 hours. (See map page 155.)

This part of the forest was once a vast stretch of water used by migrating birds, hence the name 'Pool of the Birds'.

Start on foot from the ruined Maison Marose, alongside the N808, proceeding north, crossing the first forest track and turning left along the next, broad one, in the direction of the Etoile crossroads.

Near the route stands a large beech tree, now rather dilapidated from lightning strikes and old age, but once an important landmark, possibly used for hanging wrong-doers.

At the Mare aux Oies crossroads, look for the track off right which, after about 500m, turns 90° right, continues over one stream and crosses another near the L'Ermitage farm clearing. Veering right again, the route crosses a tributary and a forest track, before joining the broad track from the Etoile crossroads reached on the outward leg. Now simply walk south back to the start.

Château de Tesse-la-Madeleine, near Bagnoles

ROUTE 4: BAGNOLES-DE-L'ORNE TO ST MICHEL-DES-ANDAINES — PROMENADE DU ROCHER BROUTIN

5km; 3$^1/_2$ hours.

The walk starts from the Place du Marché in the north of Bagnoles-de-l'Orne. Take the stony road north-west along-side the railway line, curving round to the St Ortaire priory. Cross the railway, walk along the N386 for 200m then turn right into the forest at the first picnic area, following yellow waymarks as the walk crosses several forest tracks. (Any of these lead in a short distance to St Michel, where a bus may be taken back to Bagnoles; or the walk can be reversed to give a longer outing.)

The Rocher Broutin rises from the forest plateau in La Ferté-Macé section and provides panoramic views over neighbouring villages and La Ferté-Macé itself. The name Broutin is associated with several local people: Jean Broutyn, a notable military officer of the seventeenth century; Gabriel Broutyn, a forestry officer; and Guillaume Broutyn, in 1783 an early 'Chancellor of the Exchequer'.

ROUTE 5: CIRCUIT OF L'ETANG-DE-LA-FORGE

3km; 1 hour 15 minutes. (See map page 155.)

The forges of La Sauvagère, which thrived in the seven-teenth century, used this convenient stretch of water, local ore and virtually limitless timber in the adjacent forest.

Starting from Carrefour de la Forge, north of St Michel-des-Andaines, walk west along the forest road overlooking the Vée valley, with views towards La Sauvagère. At the top of the hill, take the Mont-Albert forest road sharp left, cross one track and at the next wide one, turn left again, returning to the start.

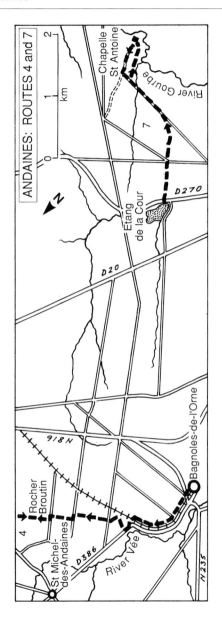

ROUTE 6: CIRCUIT DU VENEUR

3km; 1 hour 15 minutes. (See map page 155.)

From Carrefour du Veneur, proceed west and in 100m turn right in forest, reaching a track at right-angles. Turn left and immediately right, making two more 90° turns to form a circuit before rejoining the track and returning by the same way to the start. During the 'circuit' section of the walk, an extraordinary cluster of seven oak trees emanating from one root system will be passed, called the Sept Frères.

The gatehouse, Château de Carrouges

ROUTE 7: PROMENADE DE LA CHAPELLE ST ANTOINE

$6^1/_2$km; $3^1/_2$ hours. (See map page 159.)

Start at the car park on the N270 by Etang de la Cour. A stream is followed near the forest edge and the second track taken left after about 2km. This is the Sommière de Grand Magny which crosses another stream, soon after which a path leads right down to the chapel on the banks of the River Gourbe.

    Documents from Troarn abbey reveal that this Hermitage

MAIN FEATURES OF INTEREST IN THE BAGNOLES-DE-L'ORNE AREA

Bagnoles-de-l'Orne

•A fashionable spa town on the River Vée — 'Great Spring' gushing at 11,000 gallons per hour at 27°C.

•Town-centre lake is surrounded by pleasant gardens and flanked by a large casino.

•There are good shops and many sporting facilities, including tennis, boating, golf, shooting, swimming, fishing, riding and walking.

•Numerous hotels and restaurants.

La Ferté-Macé

•Less expensive than Bagnoles! (6km north). An old, cobbled town famous for its local 'tripe-en-brochette' delicacy.

•There is a Municipal Museum and a Thursday market.

Forêt des Andaines

•A major amenity area to the north-west and south-east, with 32km of metalled roads and many more forestry tracks for riding and walking.

•Several stretches of water include L'Ermitage, La Forge, La Cour and Prise Pontin.

• Rocky outcrops are found at Mont-en-Gerome, Roche aux Loups and Rocher Broutin.

•In the forest are the chapels of St Ortaire, St Antoine, Friches and Ste Geneviève.

NEARBY PLACES TO VISIT

Domfront (22km west of Bagnoles)

•Medieval town on a long, rocky ridge above the River Varenne, at the heart of the 'bocage'.

•Half-timbered houses; walls of castle keep and rampart towers provide fascinating views over narrow streets, old roofs and gateways.

•Notre-Dame-sur-l'Eau by the river is well worth seeing. Dating from 1050, it is a beautiful little cruciform Romanesque church of sublime proportions, despite being altered when the new road was built in the last century.

•Within a radius of 10km are some forty manor-houses dating back to the fifteenth and sixteenth centuries, set in picturesque farmland.

Carrouges (17km east of La Ferté-Macé)

•The centre for Parc Régional Normandie-Maine, and a small but attractive village. Information on all outdoor activities is obtainable from the office in the Maison du Parc.

•A kilometre south of the village stands Château de Carrouges, an outstanding sixteenth-century building set in tree-dotted parkland near the River Udon and surrounded by a moat. It has towers, pepperpot roofs, Renaissance windows and lovely formal gardens with avenues of chestnut trees. Guided tours are available of the opulent interior with a portrait gallery and fine furnishings. Though state-run, the château is quiet and unspoilt.

de la Herandière, as it was then known, was already in existence in 1232, and for centuries was occupied by a succession of hermits who came to find solitude and pay homage to St Antoine. Devastated during the French Revolution, it was not until 1875 that the Magny community could repossess the chapel and restore it.

From the chapel, follow a track parallel to the approach path, back to the Sommière de Grand Magny and return either by the same route or, extending the distance, via Carrefour de la Patte d'Oie and Carrefour du Grand Evier (allow an extra half an hour).

7 Brittany

How to get there

Nearest airports: Perros-Guirec, St Brieuc, Brest, Lorient and Rennes.

Rail: Links to St Brieuc and Lannion from St Malo and Roscoff (channel ports) also from Paris via Rennes.

Road: A11 Autoroute west from Paris and N12 west from St Brieuc. The D786 coast road and D788 'Corniche Bretonne' from Perros-Guirec to Trébeurden.

Area map: I.G.N. Carte Topographique, sheet 14.

Brittany is France's farthest-flung western outpost, a region softened by its proximity to the Atlantic Ocean, whose influence keeps winter temperatures as mild in places as the Côte d'Azur. Of all its many attractions, the coastline is perhaps the most memorable. Indented, immensely rugged with numerous offshore islands, the ancient underlying Armorican rock has been eroded and shaped by the elements into an infinitely varied topography.

Such a seaboard is not always kind to those who sail by, and more than one major oil spillage has threatened flora, fauna and the livelihoods of coastal communities in recent years. Inland, the equable climate encourages early vegetables, many of which find their way across the English Channel into British kitchens.

Most of Brittany's $2\frac{1}{2}$ million inhabitants are sufficiently law-abiding   not to advocate independence for their region other than by peaceful means, but a hard core of extremism does exist, not unlike Basque separatism: signs are met, here and there, of a restless urge to assert the Breton culture and gain political autonomy.

Brittany is an ancient land, liberally sprinkled with prehistoric remains, many of which simply stand unnoticed in fields or village corners. Its church architecture is rich and surprisingly delicate considering the difficulties of working with granite.

Picturesque, traditional Breton costume is still worn by some older folk, and on special occasions by youngsters too, especially the women's starched lace headdresses called *coiffes*. At *pardons* — timeworn, centuries-old expressions of religious fervour — church ceremonies are followed by processions with costumes, banners, candles and effigies of saints; later there are festivities with music and dancing. Any local pardon is worth making a special visit to see.

Many parts of Brittany lend themselves admirably to walking. Long-distance footpaths criss-cross the region

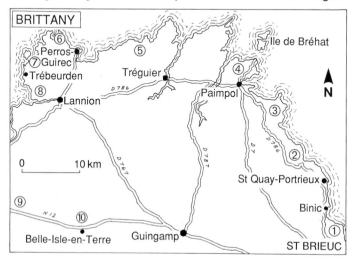

and in places hug the coast. Inland, fields are bounded by wooded banks, while elsewhere, heath and moorland carpeted with gorse rise to rocky crests. Forests are also widespread and a number of rivers flow through verdant valleys to coastal estuaries.

The following walks have been chosen for their special representation of the Breton landscape. Some pass ancient standing stones, others thread coves and beaches on the famous 'Pink Granite Coast', others still cross the rural hinterland, with its old churches and farmsteads. Paths are well waymarked, often being on parts of longer-distance routes using the familiar red and white paint flashes, and use is made too of quiet country lanes.

The weather in summer is mild, occasionally very warm, usually varied, so waterproofs and a spare sweater will not go amiss, especially on some of the longer coastal stretches. Emergency energy rations might well be advisable too, to offset the chance of cafés or shops being closed.

Traditional lace 'coiffes'

ROUTE 1: ST LAURENT-DE-LA-MER TO BINIC

16km; about 5 hours. A varied clifftop walk with numerous climbs and drops, from the coastal outskirts of St Brieuc passing several small beach resorts. Waymarked GR34. Return by bus or prearranged private transport.

St Brieuc is the busy commercial and administrative capital of Côtes-du-Nord department, situated some 3km from the coast on a plateau between the Gouédic and Gouët rivers. It is in every sense a city, with high-rise buildings and broad boulevards, but it still clings to its market-town origins and there is a fascinating old quarter grouped round an unusual twelfth-century fortified cathedral. The city is unlikely to attract holidaymakers itself, though the authorities have done much to develop amenities for the visitor. As well as hotels, restaurants and entertainment, there is a popular water-sports location with good beaches and walks out at St Laurent-de-la-Mer. It is from this seaward end of the city that the walk begins.

From the northern end of the quaysides in Le Légué, just east of St Brieuc, leave the road rising left towards La Ville Ains and Couvran and walk along a street leading towards the lighthouse. Climb steps on the left and take the old Customs Track right; near the car park are good views over St Brieuc Bay.

Follow the Anse aux Moines path and Rue des Trois-Plages and turn down to the shoreline, walking left to the promenade. At the end, take a street left, then the Chemin St Jean right, to reach Rue du Docteur-Violette, along which go left and then right on a track adjacent to the 'Centre Hélio-Marin'. Leave the track after about 500m for a path right with wide views over Plérin, just inland, the harbour entrance of Légué, St Brieuc city and Yffinias cove. The sometimes narrow path leads out past steep cliffs to Pointe du Roselier, with its car park and extensive views.

Continue west on the cliff path to Martin-Plage, ignoring paths down right to the beach and nearby properties —

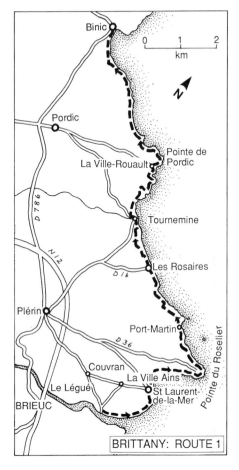

BRITTANY: ROUTE 1

taking care on this rather crumbly and eroded section. At Martin-Plage, walk up the road towards Port-Martin for 400m, then turn right on a track and left on to a cliff path. Passing through a fence, the route carries on along the cliffs before descending to the shoreline. Follow the fence again, then a wall, to the promenade at Les Rosaires. The fine beach is cradled by high wooded cliffs and there are cafés and a restaurant.

At the far end of the promenade, walk along the last

WHAT TO SEE IN
ST BRIEUC

•The massive thirteenth- to fourteenth-century cathedral of St Stephen, with turrets, towers, pepperpot roofs and a restored, austere interior. There are many ancient houses in nearby hillside Rue Fardel, including the Hôtel des Ducs de Bretagne, wherein James II sheltered after his deposition in 1688 from the English throne.

•Nearby is a beautiful fifteenth-century portico over the old Fontaine de Notre-Dame. A small museum is housed in the Town Hall.

•There are good walks in most directions from the town centre, often providing wide views, especially from 'Tèrtre Aubé' hill.

•The canalised River Gouët runs east to the tiny port of La Légué; farther on begins a sequence of beaches and small resorts, all offering bathing and water sports.

•On 31 May each year is St Brieuc's *pardon* of Notre-Dame-d'Espérance and on 29 September a lively Michael-mas Fair.

street on the left, then turn right along Rue des Horizons which continues as a path for some 2km, up and over to Tournemine (campsite and car access). Here, take Rue Ronsard to its far end, then the road left for 50m, after which turn right on a track and continue on the path opposite, past a viewpoint back over Tournemine village.

Keep along the coastline and at a crossroads, go right, soon on a path leading left into a small wood and out to a car park. Ignoring paths right, down to the shore, proceed on the cliff path and down into a steep valley at Port-Madec. Cross the stream and take the second path left (not the plainer first path) to some houses, turning right into Binic.

ROUTE 2: ST QUAY-PORTRIEUX TO BREHEC

17km; about 5 hours. A cliff top walk along unspoilt coast, round several small headlands and bays. Waymarked GR34. A linear route requiring return by bus or prearranged private transport.

St Quay-Portrieux is a centre from which fish and early vegetables are sent over to England. Once a deep-sea fishing base, its boats now concentrate on lobsters, especially around the Roches de St Quay. In common with most resorts of its size on this coast, St Quay is popular with French families. Of its four beaches, Plage de St Quay is the liveliest and has a casino and sea-water swimming pool.

Climb the steps by the casino and follow the cliff path to Pointe de l'Isnain. More steps lead to a surfaced track but this is left almost immediately for a path winding along the cliff side (ignore turnings off left and right), and leading to the beach and renovated eighteenth-century chapel at

St Quay-Portrieux

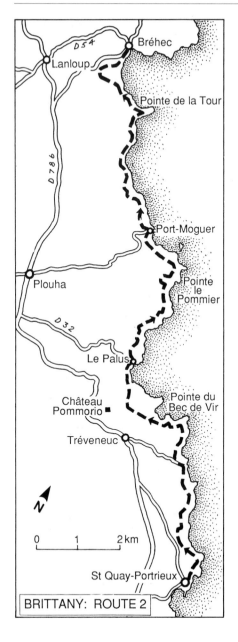

BRITTANY: ROUTE 2

St Marc. (25 minutes walk to the west lies Tréveneuc village with shops and refreshment, also a picturesque church and delightful parkland round Château Pommorio.)

Take a track right and where it bends left our route follows a path right, leading out round Pointe du Bec de Vir. Watch for a path at the right end of the car park (ignore steps down to the beach) and continue alongside private fields. Go right as far as the second crossroads and take a sunken lane opposite a road, beyond which an earth track drops to the beach at Le Palus (café and campsite).

From the car park, go up steps to the right of the café and climb through pine trees

---

WHAT TO SEE IN
GUINCAMP, 25KM WEST

•A charming old market town on the River Trieux, with narrow streets and old gabled houses, mainly fifteenth-century. Its medieval walls and fifteenth-century castle are partly intact and there is a splendid Gothic and Renaissance Basilica of Notre-Dame-de-Bonsecours.

•Guingamp is the scene of one of Brittany's great *pardons* on the first Saturday in July. There is traditional costume, music, a candle-lit procession at the three-tiered fountain (*La Plomée*) in Place du Centre, and much merry-making.

---

away from the coast, turning right to rejoin the cliff edge. At a house, turn right to Pointe de Plouha, an attractive viewpoint.

Keeping close to the coast edge, the path rounds Pointe le Pommier and emerges on to a metalled lane. Turn right for a short diversion out to Pointe de Gwin Zégal, retracing steps and continuing west to Port-Moguer beach. Our route now climbs ahead and after passing the second house, turns right to a *stèle*, commemorating the departure point of World War II pilots for Britain. In 2km, a narrow path descends to the car park at Plage Bonaparte.

From here, climb inland and turn sharp right, proceeding thereafter along the cliffs to Pointe de la Tour. The route drops to the shore, crosses a stream bed and ascends left into a wood, soon becoming an earth track along fields with views of Bréhec harbour and beach ahead. At a road junction by a Calvary, turn right along a metalled lane, and 200m after a holiday camp, take a path left to steps leading down to Bréhec beach. The resort offers accommodation, eating places, shops and buses and is pleasantly situated at the back of a deep bay.

ROUTE 3: BREHEC TO ST RIOM

12km; $3^1/_2$-4 hours. A walk round rocky headlands and small bays, culminating in Pointe de Plouézec promontory. Waymarked GR34. Return on minor roads can be made, adding 7km to the walk; or by prearranged private transport.

Starting the walk on an old Customs track from behind a newsagent's shop at Bréhec beach, the cliff edge is soon reached. At the first promontory, continue ahead to a scenic road; take this for about 1km — a short detour can be made for good views to the small headland of Beg Min Rouz. A path, right, leads down to Porz Pin, a beach made from curiously blue shingle. Cross the car park and road and find a path up on to the cliffs, veering left to the highest point. Aiming now for a conifer plantation, pass right round a fence to a stony track and along to a tarred road. This leads out (optionally) to Pointe de Minard — about 500m each way for magnificent views south and east.

Walk north-west along a stony track, over a junction to a path right which flanks fields and moorland, crosses an overgrown lane and drops to Porz Donan beach on a steep path. The way ahead now climbs in gorse, becoming a cart track alongside fields and less distinct on the ground for a stretch; it reaches a metalled road at L'Armorizel. Turn right along it towards Pointe de Plouézec, with its *table d'orientation*. Views are exceptionally wide-ranging from this prominent headland in clear weather.

Retracing steps, descend right opposite a sign 'Plage de Nothoret' over moorland. At the car park, take the road right to Port-Lazo and thence climb inland to the crossroads in St Riom (café and shop).

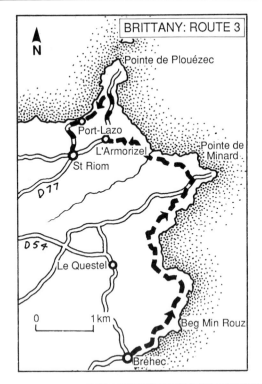

On the Iles Bréhat

ROUTE 4: PAIMPOL TO
POINTE DE L'ARCOUEST

10km; 2^1/$_2$-3 hours. This walk follows a more settled stretch of coast with several fishing harbours, views of offshore islands and the opportunity to finish with a short excursion to the lovely Iles de Bréhat. Waymarked GR34. Return by prearranged private transport.

During the nineteenth century, Paimpol expanded rapidly in association with fishermen from Iceland and Newfoundland, its story told in the novels of the French writer Pierre Loti. Today, large-scale oyster cultivation is replacing some of the prosperity enjoyed by the port in the days when its deep-sea fleet fished for cod on the Icelandic banks. There is, too, inshore fishing, pleasure boating and a thriving market for early vegetables.

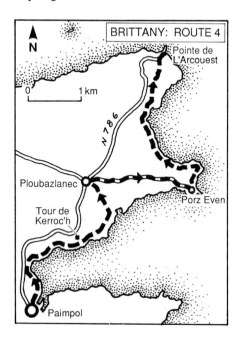

Walk along the dry-dock at the left of Paimpol's harbour, then round the back of the deep bay to Château des Salles. The route follows the shoreline, passing Tour de Kerroc'h up to the left, which can be visited. Take a narrow tarred lane continuing straight ahead, past the first cross-roads, then at a Calvary go left, cross the D789 and reach the church at the centre of Ploubazlanec. There is a wall in the cemetery dedicated to Icelanders who drowned at sea.

Opposite the cemetery, turn right, cross the D789 again and continue ahead, passing the Perros Hamon chapel. In 2km, the route arrives at Porz Even, a small harbour, re-nowned for its associations with Icelandic fishermen, well worth exploring. Take a small path on the north side of the harbour, leading to La Trinité chapel, whereafter it climbs left to La Croix des Veuves.

Walk along the metalled road west from here, and at an electricity transformer, go right down to the *grève* (bay) of Launay. Turn right on a road, then left along the shore for 500m, finally climbing inland. Turn right on to a broad path, then left through broom, continuing along a stony track. When a road is reached, turn right and at the first cross-roads, turn left then right on to an earth track to arrive at the landing stage at Pointe de l'Arcouest.

From Porz Even onwards, views over the multitude of offshore islets are fascinating and from Pointe de l'Arcouest itself, frequent 10-minute crossings are made to Iles de Bréhat — two pink-granite islands joined by a neck of land. They are well worth a visit: an intimate landscape of tiny walled fields and villas, dotted with fig trees, oleander, myrtle and mimosa, all of which flourish in the mild climate.

ROUTE 5: PLOUGRESCANT TO KERGONET

9km; 3 hours. An easy walk, part on lanes, part on the
waymarked GR34 coast path, round a pleasant estuary
headland.

Plougrescant stands near the entrance to the River Jaudy
which runs upstream to Tréguier, some 14km distant by
road. That town is the birthplace of the French writer Ernest
Renan and also contains a beautiful granite cathedral and
cloisters, dating from the thirteenth century. Nearby is the
village of Minihy-Tréguier, scene of a particularly colourful
Breton *pardon* on 19 May each year.

   History tells us that St Gonéry, who lived for much of his
life in central Brittany during the sixth century, came to Plougrescant to die. His tomb is situated in a rather odd-looking
chapel with a tilting steeple; inside the nave are interesting paintings from the fifteenth and sixteenth centuries.
Each springtime, a boat ritually carries the saint's reliquary
on to Ile Loaven, 3km away, where his mother, Elibou-
bane, lies buried.

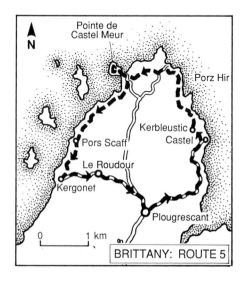

WHAT TO SEE AT TREGUIER

•A terraced town on a hill at the confluence of the rivers Guindy and Jaudy.

•Its principal sight is the magnificent granite Gothic cathedral, one of Brittany's finest ecclesiastical structures. From Place du Martray in the town centre, the cathedral's spire rises over 60m. The interior is equally impressive, with 68 windows, and cloisters giving excellent views of the building's three towers.

•In the square outside the cathedral is a statue of Ernest Renan, perhaps France's greatest rationalist writer: his seventeenth-century, half-timbered family home, where he was born in 1823, houses a museum dedicated to his life and work.

From Plougrescant, which is slightly inland, take the road towards Beg Vilin and Castel which winds down to the shoreline and continues along it for about $2^1/_2$km, with good estuary views, to just before Kerbleustic. Here, go right on a track by a house leading to the sea, and follow the shore to a large rock, where turn left back to the road. Turn right, passing in front of the Porz Hir hotel and out to Pointe de Porz Hir. Walk alongside meadowland by the shore and then along the road inland a little. At a group of farms, go right on to a recently surfaced track, round to the road and out to Pointe de Castel Meur (about 1km extra).

Proceed south-west on the shingle beach, round a white-gabled house built against a large rock and back along the shingle, continuing thereafter on a shoreline path to Pors Scaff. Where a track right, with two subsequent changes of direction, leads to a lane at Kerloquin, go straight on to Kergonet. The walk can now be concluded easily by walking inland south-east through the village of Le Roudour, back to Plougrescant on minor roads (about 2km).

ROUTE 6: PERROS-GUIREC TO KERGUNTUIL

17km; about 6 hours. A walk of exceptional quality and diversity along the amazing 'Pink Granite Coast', through several small resorts and ending at a neolithic burial site. Waymarked GR34, except at end. Return by prearranged private transport or bus.

Perros-Guirec forms an ideal base from which to explore western Brittany and is correspondingly popular, though happily its layout disperses holidaymakers and prevents any real sense of overcrowding, even in high summer. The town itself occupies a wooded headland and its best bathing beaches face north. There is also a sheltered marina, while a large artificial lake offers safe conditions for children.

Perros-Guirec's pink granite Romanesque church is one of the most beautiful in Brittany. Trestraou beach, a crescent of gently-shelving white sand, is backed by modern hotels, a casino and conference centre. It faces towards the Sept Iles, an offshore nature reserve and a sanctuary

Pink granite rock formations at Trégastel-Plage

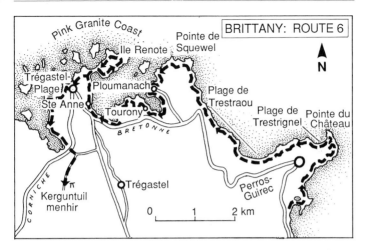

for seabirds such as cormorants, puffins, oyster-catchers and gannets. An old Customs path, one of many Sentiers des Douaniers on the French coast, encircles the Ploumanach peninsula and it is on this that our route runs.

From the dock and adjacent lake, walk north on the D786, then right on the Trestrignel road. In about 100m, turn right into a cul-de-sac to the beach, walk along it left, up the steps and turn left, then right into Rue de Pré-St Maur. Climb for 500m to the crossroads and take Rue Maurice-Denis right, out to Pointe du Château, with its *table d'orientation* viewpoint.

Now drop to Trestrignel beach and continue on the promenade, along La Messe lane and Rue Anatole-France on the left. The route proceeds via Rue des Sept Iles and Rue Maréchal-Foch on the right, to reach Trestraou beach. Walk along this lovely strand and continue ahead on Rue de la Clarté. At a big bend, turn right on the Sentier des Douaniers and walk past a maze of rocks, coves and boulders, round Pointe de Squewel with its square light-house, all part of a kind of reserve — a Parc Municipal. For this denotes the start of an extraordinary stretch of coastline — 20km or so of 'Pink Granite Coast' west to Trébuerden. Creeks and sandy coves alternate with caves, lagoons and rock pools, but it is the weathered granite

which holds the attention. Bulbous, undercut forms rise
from the sea, smoothed and shaped by waves and rain into
the most unlikely forms. Some rock groups have been
given names such as Napoleon's Hat, the Corkscrew and
the Witch.

Before continuing, note the twelfth-century oratory of
St Guirec, above the small beach. A granite statue has re-
placed the original wooden one, into the nose of which
unmarried girls once pushed needles: if the needle stuck,
marriage was imminent!

Leave on the path in front of the chapel — Bastille Promenade — which leads round to Ploumanach's port, a somewhat vulgarised scene in contrast to the natural attractions
of the coast nearby. Take the seawall along to the D786
road, turn right alongside the harbour, right again, then
left into Tourony. The route now proceeds north and west
round a sports ground and, if the tide is low enough, along
the shore to Ste Anne. (Otherwise, use the D786 and a
track right, to Ste Anne's quay).

Walk north up the main street and on to the first track
right. A detour east is possible, via a jetty, to look round
Ile Renote, adding 2km. Following the route round west to
reach Coz Porz beach, another — perhaps the best —
location is found for exploring the incredible pink granite
rock formations. Walk to La Grève Blanche and keep to the
coast for about 2km beyond the point, crossing a stream.
Turn left on the road, then right on a path past a field, and
through a farmyard. Keep along the shore for 100m and
take a stony track to the D786.

The Trégastel area is rich in prehistory and the walk ends
at a notable neolithic site. To reach it, leave the GR34 coast
path, taking instead to the road going south-east and turning right at a junction after about 500m. 1km down this
lane leads to Kerguntuil, an impressive neolithic dolmen
and *allée couverte* (mass burial chamber) in very good con-
dition. On the granite surface inside are sculptures resem-
bling nine pairs of women's breasts, apparently evoking
the mother-goddess. Excavations have revealed vases
similar to others found in Denmark and, recently, in Holland.

THE MAIN SIGHTS TO SEE ON THE 'PINK GRANITE COAST'

•An overall view can be gained from the 28km 'Corniche Bretonne' which runs from Perros-Guirec to Trébeurden — a succession of creeks, lagoons, pools, caves and large weathered rocks of astonishing colour and form.

Perros-Guirec
•A popular headland resort with good bathing beaches and a sheltered little port Good views from Pointe du Château on the peninsula's tip. There are frequent summer boat trips to Les Sept Iles, a sanctuary for bird species such as cormorants, gannets, puffins, oyster catchers and gulls.

•A *Sentier des Douaniers* (old Customs Patrol Path) runs out round the Ploumanach peninsula and provides close views of the extraordinary pink, vermillion and grey, sea-sculpted rocks.

Trégastel-Plage
•Site of some of the 'Pink Granite Coast's' most extravagant rock formations, many given names such as 'The Corkscrew', 'The Death Head' 'The Tortoises', 'Napoleon's Hat', etc.

•There is a small museum and aquarium near Coz-Pors beach.

Trébeurden
•Two family beaches separated by Le Castel isthmus and many smaller sandy bays. Good views over neighbouring wood-topped islands from Pointe de Bihit.

ROUTE 7: PENVERN AND L'ILE GRANDE

7¹/₂km; 2 hours. From a remarkable prehistoric standing stone, an easy circular walk round an offshore island connected to the mainland by a road bridge. Waymarked GR34.

About 800m south-east from the crossroads with the D788 at Pont de Penvern, stands the St Duzec menhir, a huge standing stone bordered by a Crucifixion; roughly-carved instruments of the Passion surround the figure of a woman in prayer. To see it, turn left on a path after the Café du Menhir in Penvern hamlet.

In stark contrast, only 2km away, the dome of the Pleumeur-Bodou satellite telecommunications station (guided tours for visitors) rises above the Breton heathland. It played a vital part in early intercontinental TV transmissions and the station has been developed to deal with telephone, telegraph, TV and data-transmission by satellite.

From Penvern, cross the D786 and walk along the D21 towards L'Ile Grande, with its heaths and rows of houses. On the left are another menhir and *allée couverte* (standing stone and burial chamber). Once over the bridge, turn

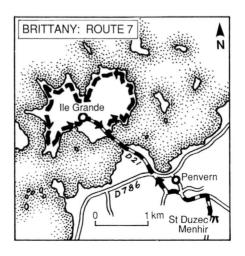

right along the shore and over rocks below residences. Pass the sailing school and continue along the coastline. Beyond Porz Gelin on the north side, a track left leads up to the highest point on the island — 35m above sea level.

The walk continues to circumnavigate the island, with good views all round, and passes the south-west corner to enter Ile Grande itself, a small township with shops, hotels and refreshment places. To return to Penvern, cross back over the bridge on the D21.

ROUTE 8: TREBEURDEN TO LANNION

16km; about 5 hours. A walk from a popular seaside resort along a coast dotted with islets and following a river inland to an interesting old market town. Waymarked GR34. Return by prearranged private transport or possibly by bus (infrequent).

Trébeurden's two main beaches, ideal for families, are separated by an isthmus leading to the rocky little peninsula of Le Castel. Also to be seen in the vicinity are a dolmen and *allée couverte* (standing stone and burial chamber), Christ chapel just north of the town centre, and Ile Milliau offshore.

Starting with a circuit of Le Castel, follow a path along the isthmus between the two beaches, walking north to south. There are magnificent views from the end in clear weather, extending to the north coast of Finistère.

Continue south along Trésmeur beach to Pointe de Bihit, whose viewing platform makes an excellent vantage point for surveying the offshore islands, many grass-covered and topped with trees. The route now turns east, alongside a field, and right, over the Pors Mabo road and along a lane ahead. In about 300m, take a stony track right, veering left on the coast path along to the Beg-Léguer car park. Climb the road opposite and carry on to a

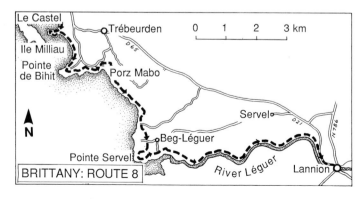

WHAT TO SEE IN AND AROUND LANNION

•The thirteenth- to fifteenth-century Brélévenez church was built by the Knights Templar on a rocky spur above the town and is reached up 142 steps: views from the terrace are excellent.

•Also in the town are many old Breton houses and pedestrianised alleyways.

•Three kilometres to the north stands the Pleumeur-Bodou Space Telecommunications Centre. In conjunction with Andover USA, and Goonhilly in Cornwall, it provides telephone and TV links between Europe and America. The station complex is large, the great 50m-high dacron sphere an incongruous intrusion on an ancient landscape scattered with 'menhirs' (standing stones). During the summer, there are guided tours, with an explanatory film and model. (**NOTE**: visits are restricted off-season).

roundabout, taking the track down right towards the sea, first in meadow then on a path round Pointe Servel.

Pass through a field and, almost immediately, go right along a track. At the second road junction turn left, then right along a wall. Walk along the edge of a grassy field and take a right turn on to a path dropping towards the River Léguer. Reaching a surfaced road, climb left and just before a bend turn off on to the riverside path which thereafter winds along the banks into Lannion.

This bustling market town of rose-granite lies at the axis of roads radiating to the coast and to numerous sites of historical interest, including castles and standing stones. The old town contains fifteenth and sixteenth century Breton houses, the church of St Jean-de-Baly only a century younger, and many pedestrianised alleyways. The church of Brélévenez, founded on an outlying spur by the Knights Templar in the twelfth century, is of great interest. It is reached up a flight of 142 steps, past old rampart terraces.

Church at Lannion

ROUTE 9: PLOUEGAT-MOYSAN TO KERLEO

12km; 4 hours. A walk in rural Brittany, past old farmsteads and over two hill viewpoints. Waymarked GR34. Return by prearranged private transport.

Plouégat-Moysan was founded originally by immigrants from Great Britain and given an important crossroads during the subsequent Roman occupation. Like much of this part of Brittany, many neolithic megaliths exists in the region.

Turn right at the *Tabac-Alimentation* shop at the village centre and drop west towards the valley, turning left to pass beneath the railway. Continue ahead over two minor junctions and over the busier N12, to reach Stivel (or St Laurent). The chapel marked on some maps is now just an ivy-clad wall, but at the crossroads there is an interesting carved cross, and a little beyond stands a curious fountain in which, it is said, local people once bathed nude to 'protect themselves against ailments of the limbs'.

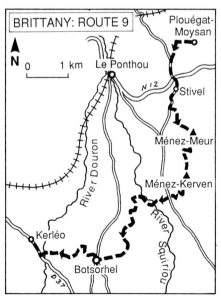

Montagnes Noires — characteristic walking country in Finistère

Still walking south, pass Quistillic farm and turn left on to a cart track, becoming a path which climbs to Menez-Meur — La Grande Montagne, though at 247m the name is relative! In clear weather, the coast is visible from Ile de Batz to Trébeurden.

The variant GR380 footpath comes in from the east, and our route now joins it going south-west off the summit (signed). Drop towards the valley, through trees, and climb to the top of Menez Kerven on path and cart track. From the 266m top it is claimed that you can see thirty-two church steeples. Leave this spot south, into meadow bordered by gorse, and go down into pine forest, emerging on to heath and dropping in zigzags to a minor road near Lézalver farm. Turn left for 10m then take a path right, past a former mill and up to the old Kerbizien farmstead, continuing on to a road.

At the road, turn left for 100m and watch for a track left leading to a field from where a track goes towards La Haie farm. Here, go left for 100m on a metalled lane and right on a broad track uphill, with wide views from the top. Turn right along the road and into the village of Botsorhel, with its

---

PARC REGIONAL
D'ARMORIQUE

•Just in Finistère, Huelgoat is an excellent centre for day walks, including the Menez-Hom hill and a Tour of the Monts d'Arrée. Further south, the coast around Concarneau and Audierne is well worth exploring. Footpaths also run out to Pointe du Raz, a French 'Land's End'.

•Any of the long-distance routes, waymarked with red and white paint flashes, can be followed for short stretches, eg GR37 east from Le Faou towards Lac de Guerlédan and on through rural Brittany's heartland to the Forêt de Paimpont-Brocéliande.

•The GR38 runs south-east from Douarnenez and can be picked up around Quimper, Gourin, Baud and Redon, with 'arms' to the coast at Quimperlé, Auray and Quiberon.

---

seventeenth-century church containing curious ancient statues.

Opposite the cemetery and by the last house at the north of the village, turn left into a field path, passing an embankment and ascending to a wood, where a track is followed left to a road. Turn right for about 200m and, beyond a house on the left, walk on a track dropping into and out of the Douron valley. Kerléo hamlet (hotel/restaurant and grocery shop) lies just to the right along the road.

ROUTE 10: BELLE-ISLE-EN-TERRE
TO GURUNHUEL

15km; 5-5$^{1}/_{2}$ hours. A varied walk across quite steeply undulating countryside and forest, passing near a very attractive Breton church. Waymarked GR34A. Return by prearranged private transport. Large-scale map useful.

Belle-Isle-en-Terre is a pleasant Breton village with hotels, restaurants, shops and a café. Walk south, following GR34A waymarks, by the River Léguer, after which take the minor road left to a mill and thereafter up a winding, stony track. At a metalled road, turn right and immediately left down by a house. This leads to a junction: 200m ahead stands Ste Jeune chapel. If visited, retrace steps to the junction and fork right on the road, forking next left and next right to Kerambastard. Go right between houses, dropping to trees and the River Léguer again, crossing it on a small bridge; go over the road and up a track into woods opposite. At a flatter clearing, go left and when a broader track is reached, left again.

Unless nearby Les Vieilles Forges is to be visited (café and campsite), the route doubles back south-east on the wide forest track after meeting the D33 road. Uphill, it is not

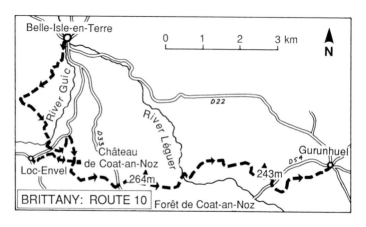

long before Château de Coat-an-Noz is reached and here
a short detour right (west) is possible, 1km each way, to
see one of the prettiest churches in the region at Loc-
Envel. Dating from the sixteenth century, it has many
interesting features inside and out, including a west façade
surmounted by an arched steeple.

The way ahead now passes south of the château and
comes out at the Maison Forestière, down on the D33 in
the Coat-an-Noz forest. Turn left and immediately right on a
forest track. After 150m, turn right again on to a narrow
path, keeping up left at a fork and eventually winding down
into trees. Cross a very broad forest track and continue
ahead to the far end of a young conifer plantation (path not
too clear on the ground), then taking a thin path through
undergrowth. Follow the widest track left, and cross the
Léguer on a wooden footbridge, right. Proceed ahead and
emerge on to a clear track, along which turn right. Shortly
afterwards, turn up sharp left.

Arriving at more level ground after 750m or so, go right,
then right again on forest tracks, then left to arrive at a
meadow and pass a house. Carry straight on along the
track ahead before turning right on a stony lane, veering
left down to the D54. Short-cutting the road fork, a metalled
lane leads south-east, and in 500m a stony track climbs left,
up hillside, bends right, passes the signed junction with the
GR341 variant and enters the village of Gurunhuel (café,
shops and restaurant).